Origami *for* everyone

A FIREFLY BOOK

Published by Firefly Books Ltd. 2011

First printing

Publisher Cataloging-in-Publication Data (U.S.)

Boursin, Didier.
   Origami for everyone / Didier Boursin.
[160] p. : col. photos. ; cm.
ISBN 978-1-55407-958-2 (bound)
ISBN 978-1-55407-792-2 (pbk.)
1. Origami. I. Title.
736.982 dc22   TT870.B687   2011

Library and Archives Canada Cataloguing in Publication

Boursin, Didier
   Origami for everyone / Didier Boursin.

ISBN 978-1-55407-958-2 (bound)
ISBN 978-1-55407-792-2 (pbk.)
  1. Origami. I. Title.
TT870.B68195 2011   736'.982   C2011-902271-0

Published in the United States by
Firefly Books (U.S.) Inc.
P.O. Box 1338, Ellicott Station
Buffalo, New York 14205

Published in Canada by
Firefly Books Ltd.
66 Leek Crescent
Richmond Hill, Ontario L4B 1H1

Printed in China

The publisher gratefully acknowledges the financial support for our publishing
program by the Government of Canada through the Canada Book Fund as
administered by the Department of Canadian Heritage.

Origami *for* everyone

Beginner • Intermediate • Advanced

Didier Boursin

FIREFLY BOOKS

Contents

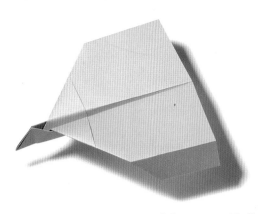

Introduction

Creating a book of paper folds takes time — and lots of it. Few people understand that it sometimes takes several months to adjust a model and its step-by-step instructions. The models are worked out meticulously, down to the smallest details.

Creating a very simple fold is actually quite complicated because I try to use a minimum of material for maximum expression. Every fold is a humorous wink at life. For each model, I invite you to appreciate the subtleties of its construction, its beauty and its gracefulness.

For many years I have tried to change origami, including the overall concept about it. Folding is an art form and a means of poetic expression. It is also a thought game that allows our nimble fingers to fold a simple sheet of paper. By its nature, it is suitable for enthusiasts of all ages. This book is the expression of a modern designer who sculpts paper, and each model is an addition to one's collection of games or gallery of paintings and drawings. I hope this book stimulates curiosity and imagination, develops creativity and brings a little happiness to every day.

I hope that you will derive as much pleasure as I do from producing these magnificent creations, which are truly small masterpieces.

Origami for Everyone includes a world of folds — charming animals, soaring airplanes, and an assortment of surprises to challenge the fingertips and delight the eyes.

Didier Boursin

Origami Tips

First of all, make yourself comfortable at a table, alone or with some friends. Start folding calmly and patiently, without getting discouraged if the fold seems difficult at first. You will not always succeed at making a model on your first attempt; usually the second try is better than the first. If you really stumble over a step, let your work sit for a few hours, or even several days. This break will often allow you to approach paper-folding with a new attitude and will get things moving again. With a little thought and focus, you will have the satisfaction of creating a paper masterpiece with your own hands. Eventually, you'll be able to fold effortlessly, practically with your eyes shut.

Levels of Difficulty ▶ ▶▶ ▶▶▶

The models in this book are divided into three sections based on level of difficulty — beginner ▶, intermediate ▶▶ and advanced ▶▶▶. Before you start making models, read pages 10–17, which explain the symbols, bases and folds used in this book.

Once you're ready to move on to the models, I suggest that you begin with the easier projects first before attempting some of the more complicated ones.

Making Folds

Before beginning a project, you should practice with ordinary paper to make some of the principal folds of origami. These include the valley fold, mountain

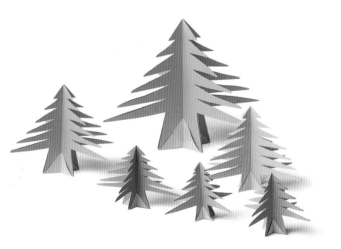

fold, pleat fold, crease, match the dots, and cuts. You will also want to try some of the more complicated folds, such as the inside reverse fold, outside reverse fold and squash fold.

Making Bases

By combining some of the folds, you will achieve the bases needed to make several of the projects in this book. In time, your fingertips will fold them automatically without your needing to look at the diagrams. Some of these bases, like the preliminary base and waterbomb base, are used for many creations; other bases, like the bird base, are used for only a few of the projects. Regardless, practicing these bases will help you to master your technique.

Diagrams

Every fold for a project is explained step by step by the outline drawings.

Carefully study the drawing as well as the explanatory text instructions. Sometimes the diagrams are broken down into smaller details (for example, feet and heads for some of the animal models). You should complete all these details before going on to the next steps. The parts in color indicate that they are the reverse of the sheet of paper.

Paper

The best papers to use for origami are those that crease well and are sufficiently strong for repeated folding and unfolding. White or colored papers that are used for photocopying or computer printing are excellent for origami. In more technical terms, paper with a 20–24 lb bond weight (between 75 and 90 grams) works well. Many arts and crafts stores carry special origami paper, as well as a variety of marbled, patterned and decorated papers. Be sure to avoid drawing paper, however, which is usually too thick for making models. Do not use paper that will tear

after being folded several times, such as tracing paper, newsprint or certain types of recycled paper. Once you have some experience making the models in this book, you'll be ready to experiment more with different types of paper.

The required paper shape is indicated at the beginning of each model: square, A4 (see page 16), letter-sized (8½ x 11), or very small. For a model made up of several pieces, use small sheets (3–4 inches) or one-quarter of an A4 or letter-sized sheet. For a one-piece model, use a larger square (8–10 inches) or a full A4 or letter-sized sheet.

For experienced folders, any size of square will work. As a general rule, it's best to start big and then work down to smaller squares as you gain practice. Some models require a strip of paper. (The dimensions are specified each time.)

Pages 16–17 cover sizes and shapes in greater detail. There you will learn how to make a square from a rectangle, a rectangle from a square, and other shapes.

Other Tools

A folding bone made from wood or plastic is helpful for making creases in certain models. The flat side of the tool is used to help define and complete the fold.

Although you may not need a folding bone, you will need a pair of scissors for cutting your base papers and for adding details to many of the creations in this book. For example, scissors may be used to make feet, ears or whiskers for some of the animal models.

Symbols, Folds and Bases

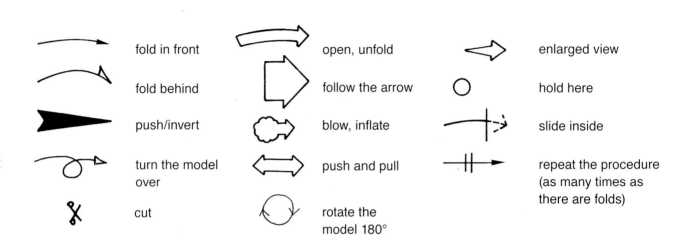

fold in front	open, unfold	enlarged view
fold behind	follow the arrow	hold here
push/invert	blow, inflate	slide inside
turn the model over	push and pull	repeat the procedure (as many times as there are folds)
cut	rotate the model 180°	

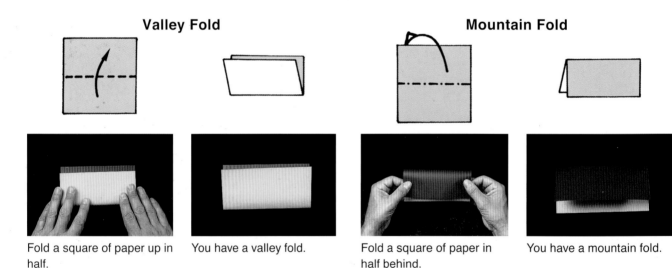

Valley Fold

Fold a square of paper up in half.

You have a valley fold.

Mountain Fold

Fold a square of paper in half behind.

You have a mountain fold.

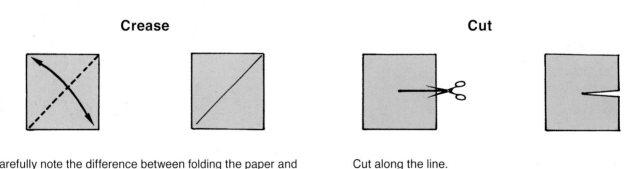

Crease

Carefully note the difference between folding the paper and creasing the paper. In the first case you keep the fold; in the second case you fold it, then unfold it.

Cut

Cut along the line.

Match the Dots (Join the Points)

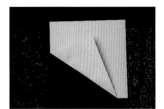

Fold one point to the spot indicated.

Flatten the fold.

Preliminary Base

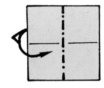

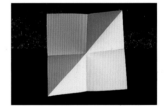
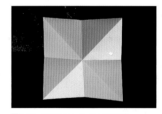

On a square sheet of paper, crease a central mountain fold.

Then crease a second central mountain fold as shown.

Crease a diagonal valley fold.

Then crease a second diagonal valley fold as shown.

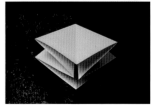

Press on the center from behind.

Grasp two opposite corners, and bring the folds together to form a diamond shape.

Flatten the entire model.

You have a preliminary base.

Waterbomb Base

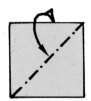

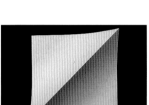 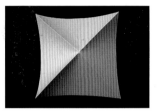 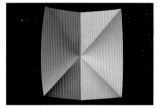 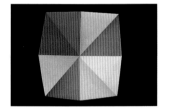

On a square sheet of paper, crease a diagonal mountain fold.

Then crease a second diagonal mountain fold as shown.

Crease a central fold in a valley fold.

Then crease a second central valley fold.

  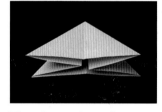

Press on the center from behind.

Grasp two opposite corners, and bring the folds together to form a triangle.

Then flatten the entire model. You have the waterbomb base.

Squash Fold

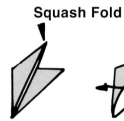

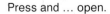

Raise to vertical.

Press and … open.

Flatten.

Inside Reverse Fold

 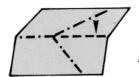 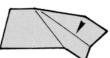

Make a valley fold, then bring the upper-right corner over as shown.

Then open.

Push down in the center to make the center fold a valley fold. Make mountain folds on either side of the center fold. Then push in the right side.

You have an inside reverse fold.

Outside Reverse Fold

Make a valley fold, then bring the lower-right corner over as shown.

Then open.

Make the center fold a valley fold. Make mountain folds on either side of the center fold. Then push in the left side.

You have an outside reverse fold.

Pleat Fold

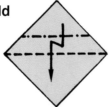 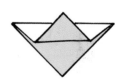

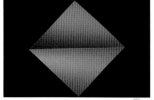 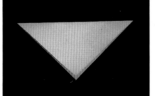 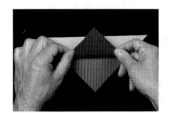 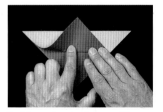

Fold a square of paper in half from the front.

You have a triangle.

Bring up one point.

Fold again as shown. You have a pleat fold.

Special Animal Bases

Fish Base:

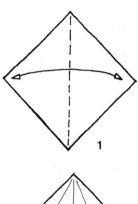 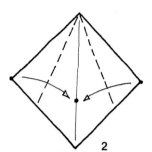 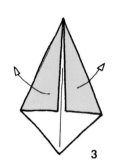 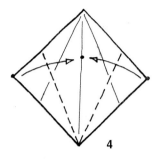

1   2   3   4

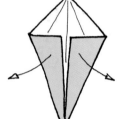 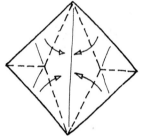  

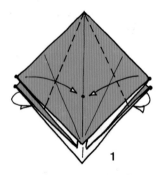

5   6   7

1 Precrease as shown, vertically.
2 Fold the upper edges toward the central fold.
3 Unfold.
4 Fold the bottom edges in the same way.
5 Unfold.
6 Refold the edges at the same time as you pinch the side points.
7 Lay the base flat, placing the points up.

Frog Base:

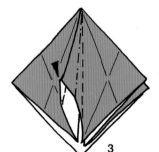 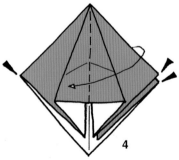

1   2   3   4

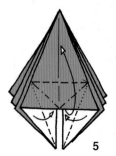 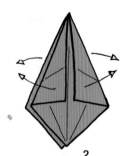 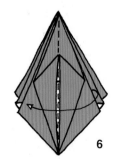 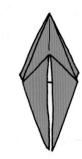

5   6

1 Fold the upper edges on both sides of a preliminary base.
2 Unfold.
3 Lift up a vertical flap, then open it by flattening.
4 Repeat the same fold with the other three flaps.
5 Lift up a layer while folding the points in half.
6 Turn a flap and repeat this fold with the other three sides.

14

Horse Base:

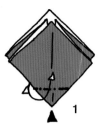

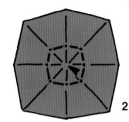

1 To make this base for the horse's belly, fold all the layers front and back, then unfold completely.

2 Mountain fold the central square, then push in its middle to sink the square.

3 In the center of the square, the diagonals are valley folds and the medians are mountain folds. Lay the base flat as in the beginning.

Bird Base:

1 Make a preliminary base, then fold the bottom edges to the central fold.

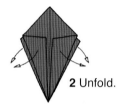

2 Unfold.

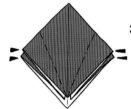

3 Push in the sides with inside reverse folds.

Birds' Legs:

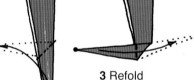

3 Refold toward the right.

4 Unfold completely.

6 Fold in half while placing the triangle's sides into a mountain fold.

1 The fold is made in two steps.

2 Fold up the point to the horizontal.

5 Mountain fold the two upper sides of the triangle, then valley fold the last point of the triangle.

Foot/Beak:

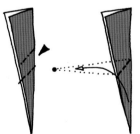

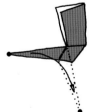

1 To achieve this fold.

2 Fold up the point to the horizontal.

3 Fold the point down. To make a beak, fold the point toward the right to lie parallel.

4 Unfold completely.

5 Mountain fold and valley fold as indicated, then fold twice toward the vertical fold.

6 Fold flat.

Shapes and Sizes

You'll find all the information here that you need to make squares and "A4" sheets. Once you're familiar with the shapes, try placing pieces alongside one another to make other shapes. Or cut the squares along fold lines and rearrange the pieces to make new designs.

Hint: You may purchase square origami paper or cut your own squares from a sheet of letter-sized or A4 paper. Origami instructions often refer to A4 paper. An A4 sheet can be made by trimming ⅝ inch from the width of a letter-sized sheet.

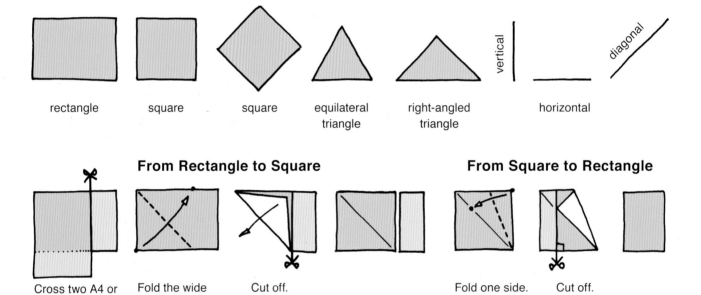

rectangle   square   square   equilateral triangle   right-angled triangle   vertical   horizontal   diagonal

From Rectangle to Square

Cross two A4 or 8½ x 11 sheets to get a square.

Fold the wide edge to the long edge.

Cut off.

From Square to Rectangle

Fold one side.

Cut off.

A4 Size

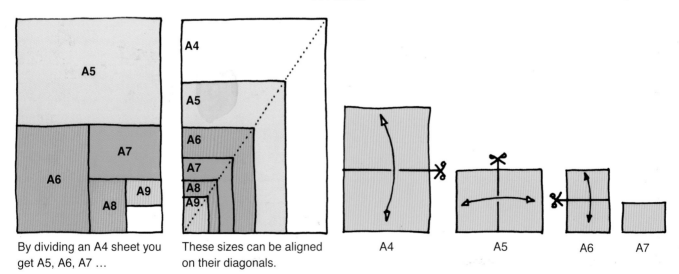

By dividing an A4 sheet you get A5, A6, A7 …

These sizes can be aligned on their diagonals.

A4   A5   A6   A7

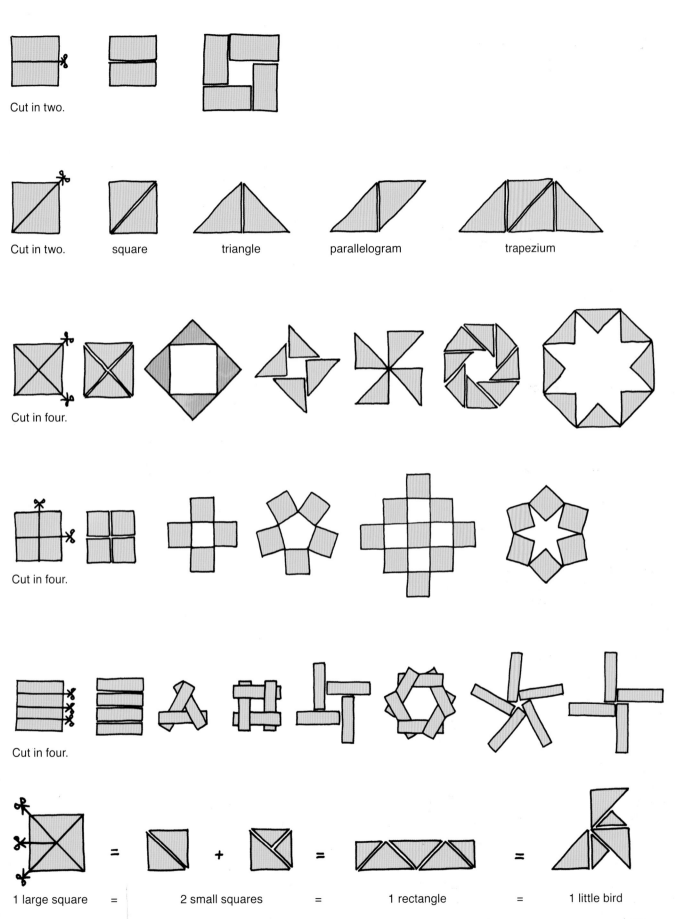

Cut in two.

Cut in two. square triangle parallelogram trapezium

Cut in four.

Cut in four.

Cut in four.

1 large square = 2 small squares = 1 rectangle = 1 little bird

Overflight

▌ Beginner

This traditional model is Japanese.
You can fly this plane over unexplored
territories because its wing flaps give it
exceptional flight stability.

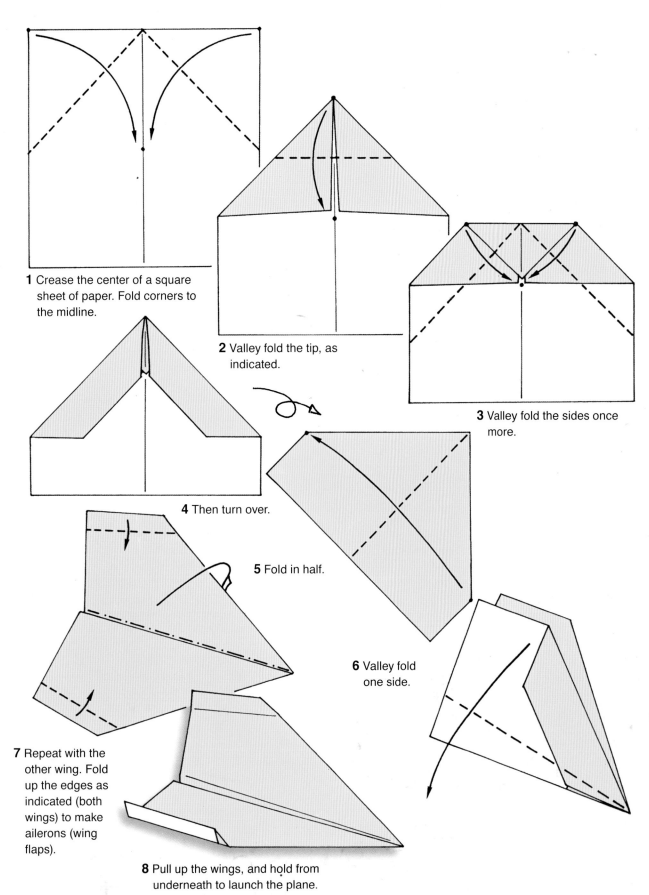

1 Crease the center of a square sheet of paper. Fold corners to the midline.

2 Valley fold the tip, as indicated.

3 Valley fold the sides once more.

4 Then turn over.

5 Fold in half.

6 Valley fold one side.

7 Repeat with the other wing. Fold up the edges as indicated (both wings) to make ailerons (wing flaps).

8 Pull up the wings, and hold from underneath to launch the plane.

Envelope

▶ Beginner

This envelope is a very practical creation. Use it to hold pictures, stamps and all your other little treasures.

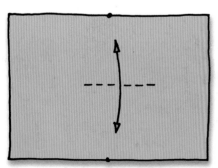
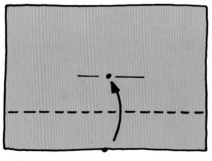
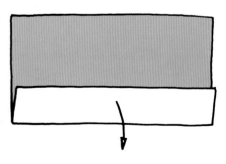

1 Partially crease the center of a letter-sized or A4 sheet (see p. 16).

2 Fold the bottom edge to the center crease …

3 … then unfold.

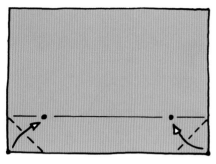

4 Fold the two corners up along the crease.

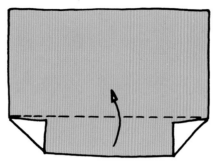

5 Fold the bottom strip back up …

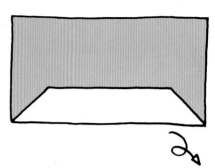

6 … Like this, then turn it over.

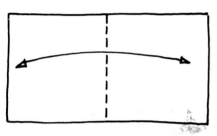

7 Crease the center.

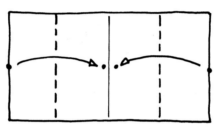

8 Fold the sides along the center crease.

Enlarged View

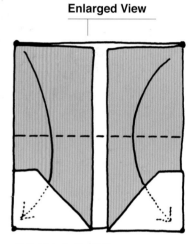

9 Fold in half, sliding corners into the pockets.

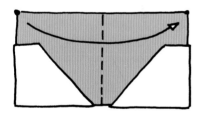

10 Fold in half.

11 The envelope has two outside pockets and …

12 … two inside pockets, as well as a large pocket when it is opened underneath.

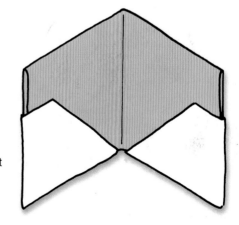

Rabbit

▶ Beginner

This naughty rabbit is nibbling on carrots in the garden. With its ears up it stands on guard, ready to bolt at the slightest noise.

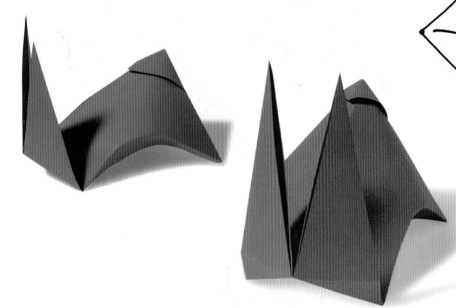

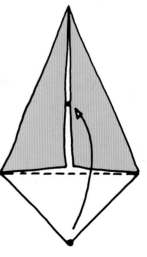

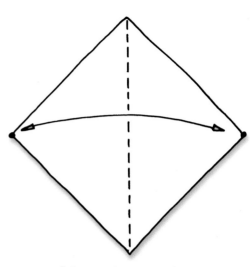

1 Crease the center of a square sheet of paper.

2 Fold the edges along the center crease.

3 Fold up the triangle.

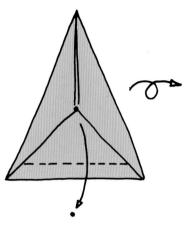

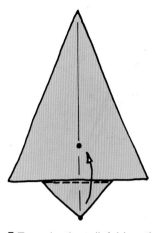

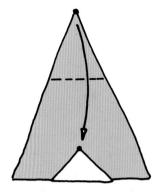

4 Make a pleat fold by bringing the triangle down. Then turn it over.

5 To make the tail, fold up the triangle.

6 To make the head, fold the point toward the bottom.

Enlarged View

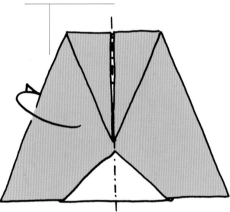

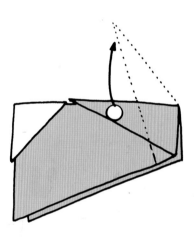

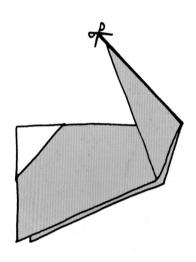

7 Fold in half.

8 Bring up the points of the ears.

9 Separate the ears by cutting them.

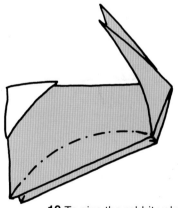

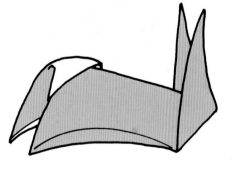

10 To give the rabbit volume, curve the sides with your thumbs.

11 The last fold gives a sense of movement to the rabbit.

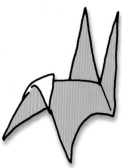

Decorations

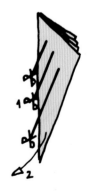

▶ Beginner

Just change the number of cuts and their
locations to create different styles of stars.
Stick these decorations on a window and
admire their beauty in the light.

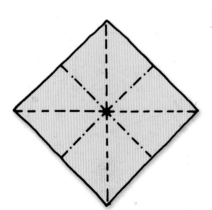

The Star

Enlarged View

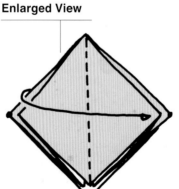

1 Start with a preliminary base
   (see p. 11).

2 Fold the entire
   model in half.

3 Make a crease by
   folding an edge over
   along the vertical edge
   (1), then cut along the
   crease through all
   layers (2).

4 Make three
   parallel cuts,
   then unfold the
   whole thing.

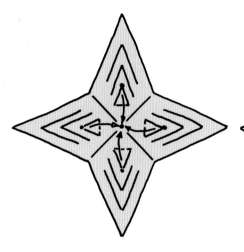

5 Fold the four small triangles toward the center.

6 Slide the four largest triangles under the first set.

7 Make all the valley and mountain creases as shown.

The Square

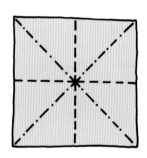

1 Start with a waterbomb base (see p. 12).

Enlarged View

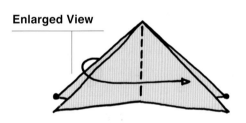

2 Fold the entire model in half.

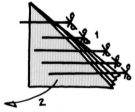

3 Make parallel cuts (1), stopping at different distances from the vertical edge. Unfold the model (2).

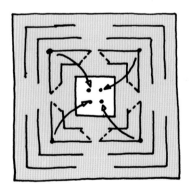

4 Fold the first four points toward the center.

5 Fold the points near the edge under the first set.

6 To flatten well, place under a pile of heavy books for several days.

Owl

> Beginner

Most owls sleep during the day, perched high up on a branch. At night, they hoot and hunt in the moonlight.

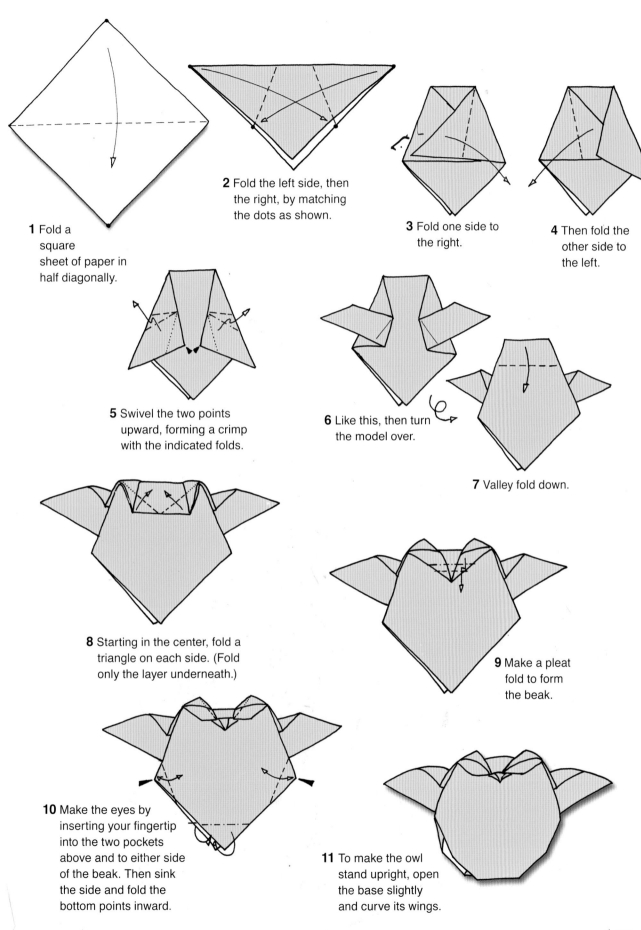

1 Fold a square sheet of paper in half diagonally.

2 Fold the left side, then the right, by matching the dots as shown.

3 Fold one side to the right.

4 Then fold the other side to the left.

5 Swivel the two points upward, forming a crimp with the indicated folds.

6 Like this, then turn the model over.

7 Valley fold down.

8 Starting in the center, fold a triangle on each side. (Fold only the layer underneath.)

9 Make a pleat fold to form the beak.

10 Make the eyes by inserting your fingertip into the two pockets above and to either side of the beak. Then sink the side and fold the bottom points inward.

11 To make the owl stand upright, open the base slightly and curve its wings.

Boat

▶ Beginner

Decorate your boat, give it a name and then launch it in the water.

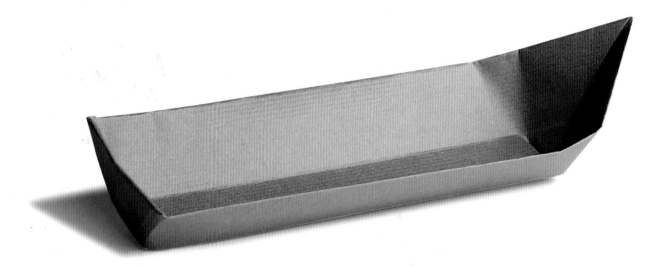

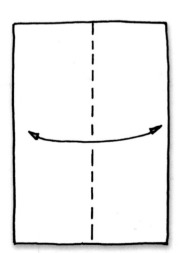

1 Crease lengthwise the center of a letter-sized or A4 sheet (see p. 16).

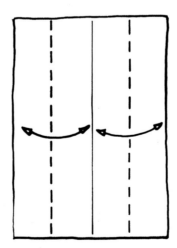

2 Crease the edges along the center.

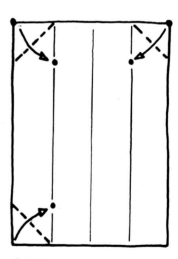

3 Fold the three corners shown.

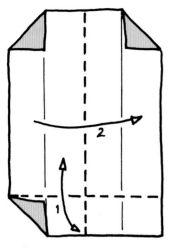

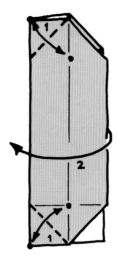

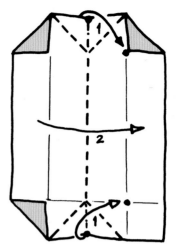

4 Crease horizontally (1) along the lower corner, then fold in half (2).

5 Crease the upper and lower corners (1), then unfold (2).

6 Pull the triangles, top and bottom (1), into inside reverse folds (see p. 13) by refolding in half (2).

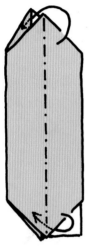

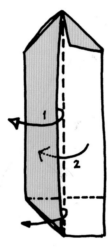

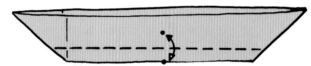

9 With the model flat, crease one third with a valley crease, then a mountain crease.

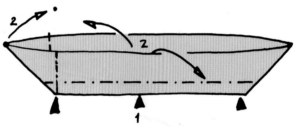

7 To lock the ends, fold the strip inside and under the different layers at both ends.

8 Open gently (1) and fold the other strip inside (2).

10 To shape the bottom of the boat, push on the lower strip (1) by clearly marking the mountain crease. Then give the boat volume by folding up the back (2).

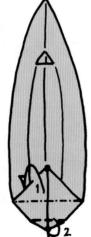

11 Fold the upper triangle (1) inside; then fold the small triangle (2) at the bottom, under.

Enlarged View

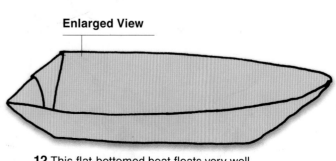

12 This flat-bottomed boat floats very well.

Dart

▶ Beginner

Among the traditional paper airplanes, the Dart is the best known model because of its simple construction, combined with its excellent flight performance.

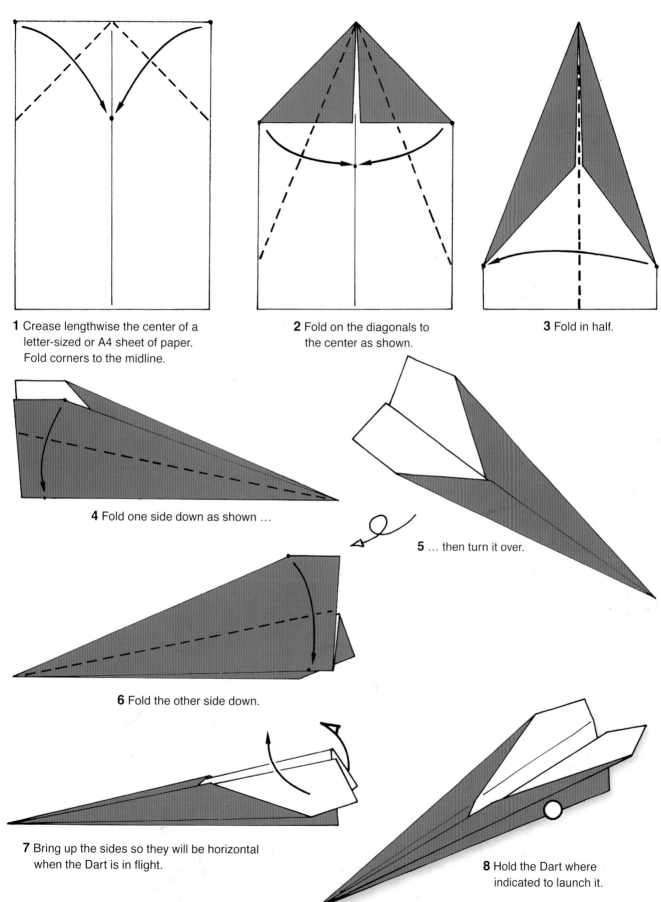

1 Crease lengthwise the center of a letter-sized or A4 sheet of paper. Fold corners to the midline.

2 Fold on the diagonals to the center as shown.

3 Fold in half.

4 Fold one side down as shown …

5 … then turn it over.

6 Fold the other side down.

7 Bring up the sides so they will be horizontal when the Dart is in flight.

8 Hold the Dart where indicated to launch it.

Whale

▶ Beginner

A whale can jump out of the water gracefully despite its weight, which can exceed 150 tons. In some species of whales, their teeth are replaced by numerous plates which filter the plankton and tiny fish that make up their diet.

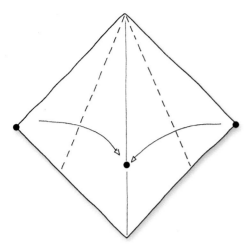

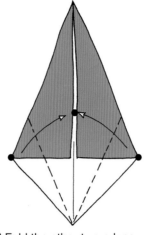

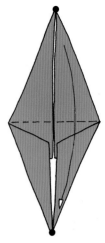

1 Starting with a square, creased on the diagonal, fold the edges to the center crease.

2 Fold the other two edges to the center.

3 Fold the top point to the bottom.

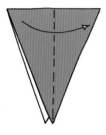

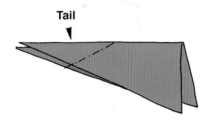

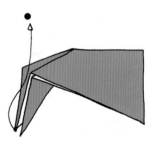

Tail

4 Fold in two.

5 Make a reverse fold after precreasing.

6 Bring one point back up with a small reverse fold.

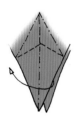

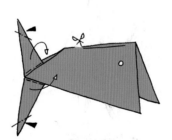

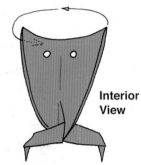

Interior View

7 Detail of the folding of the point of the tail.

8 Make small reverse folds on the tips of the tail. Cut a thin strip along the back, and fold straight up, spreading to look like a water jet. For the eyes, paper punch through all thicknesses. Turn over.

9 Round the body and tuck one side into the other.

Glider

▶ Beginner

Originally from China, this plane went from one continent to another, undergoing a few variations along the way. It flies on a perfect trajectory without any premature landings. When it does come to earth, it lands softly.

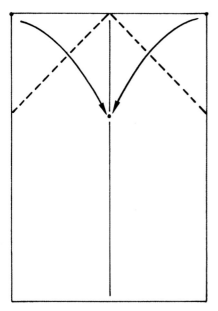

1 Crease lengthwise the center of a letter-sized or A4 sheet of paper. Fold corners to the midline.

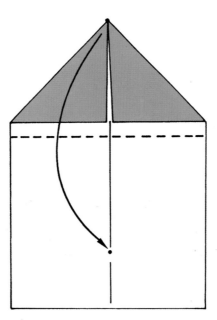

2 Valley fold the top point down onto the center line, leaving a strip as shown.

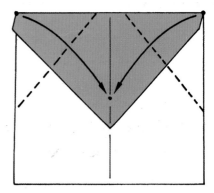

3 Then fold the points to the middle along the diagonals shown. (Folds do not meet, except at points.)

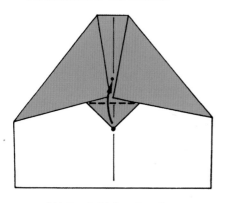

4 Valley fold the triangle up.

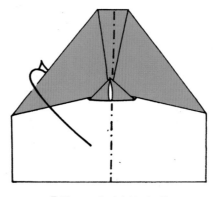

5 Mountain fold in half.

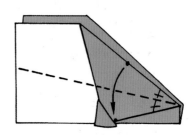

6 Fold one side down, dividing the angle in half.

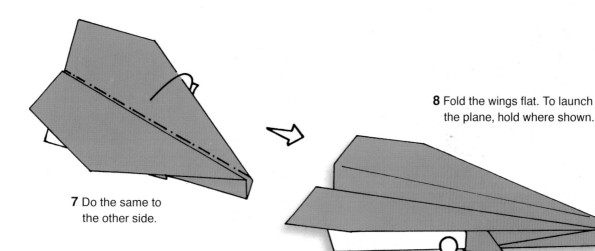

7 Do the same to the other side.

8 Fold the wings flat. To launch the plane, hold where shown.

Chopper

▶ Beginner

Antoine de Saint-Exupéry, author of *The Little Prince*, loved to fold helicopters like this one when he was between flights. He would hurl them out of windows to the great delight of children. This model returns to the principle of the original folds.

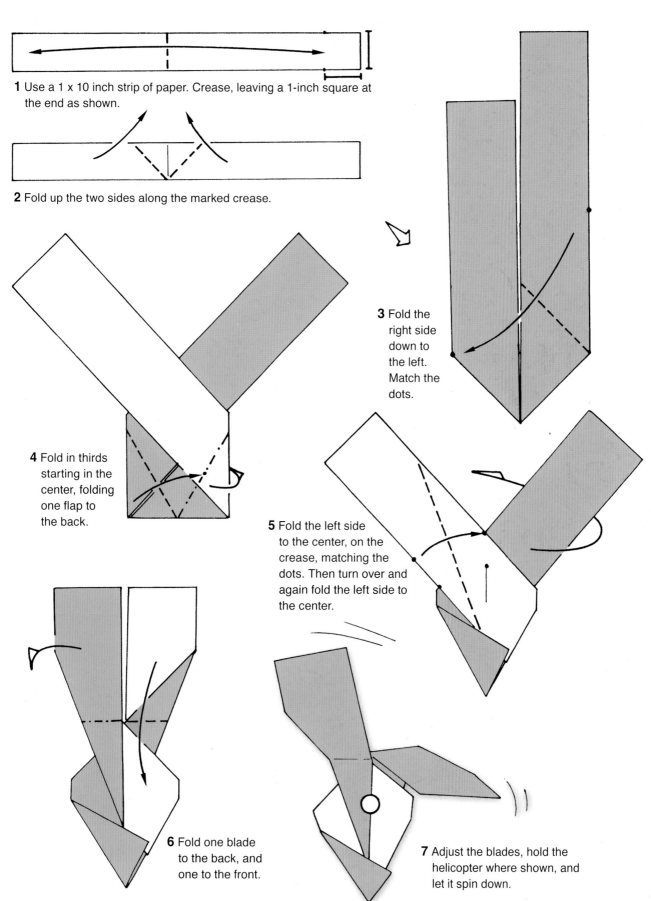

1 Use a 1 x 10 inch strip of paper. Crease, leaving a 1-inch square at the end as shown.

2 Fold up the two sides along the marked crease.

3 Fold the right side down to the left. Match the dots.

4 Fold in thirds starting in the center, folding one flap to the back.

5 Fold the left side to the center, on the crease, matching the dots. Then turn over and again fold the left side to the center.

6 Fold one blade to the back, and one to the front.

7 Adjust the blades, hold the helicopter where shown, and let it spin down.

Tube and Paper Twirler

▶ Beginner

The tube, thrown sharply out of a window away from the wall toward the horizon, will fly for about 30 feet, landing softly in the street on the opposite side. The paper twirler is simple to make, but will amaze you when you drop it from a high place: it will spin around itself as it falls.

Tube

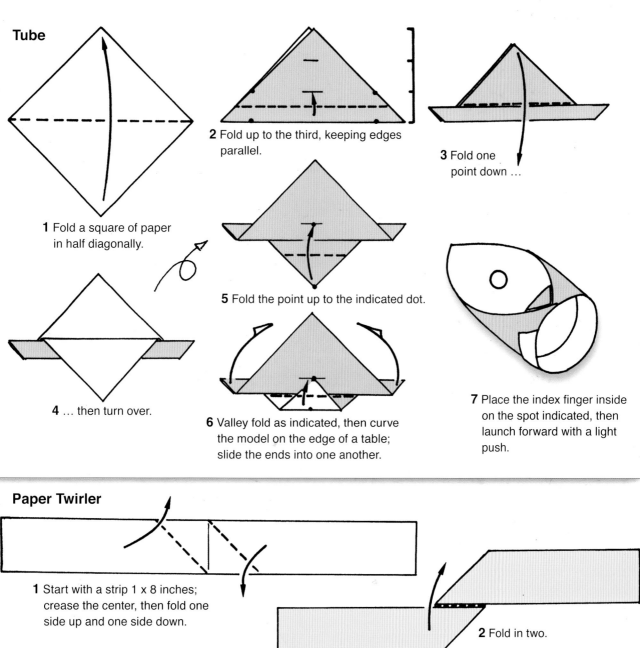

1 Fold a square of paper in half diagonally.

2 Fold up to the third, keeping edges parallel.

3 Fold one point down ...

4 ... then turn over.

5 Fold the point up to the indicated dot.

6 Valley fold as indicated, then curve the model on the edge of a table; slide the ends into one another.

7 Place the index finger inside on the spot indicated, then launch forward with a light push.

Paper Twirler

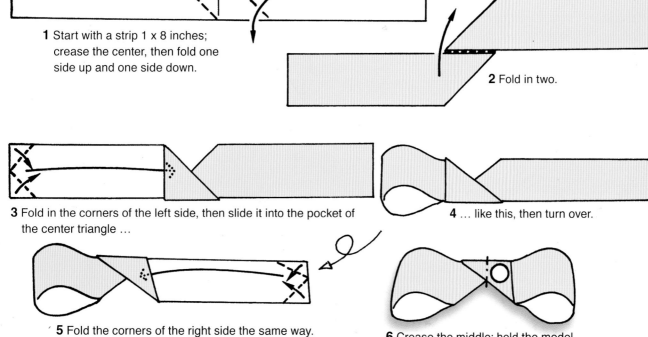

1 Start with a strip 1 x 8 inches; crease the center, then fold one side up and one side down.

2 Fold in two.

3 Fold in the corners of the left side, then slide it into the pocket of the center triangle ...

4 ... like this, then turn over.

5 Fold the corners of the right side the same way.

6 Crease the middle; hold the model vertically at the spot shown. Let go and it will fall, turning on itself.

39

Butterfly

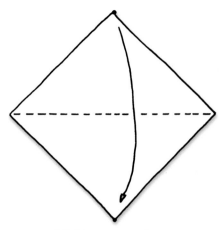

1 Fold a square of paper in half diagonally.

▌Beginner

Fold butterflies in all sizes and colors and hang them all over a room. You can also glue them to birthday cards and party invitations.

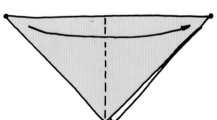

2 Fold in half again.

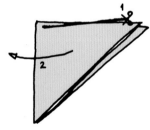

3 To make the antennae, cut the edge through all layers (1) and open (2).

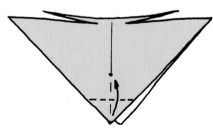

4 Fold up one layer to join the points.

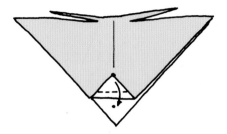

5 Make a pleat by folding the triangle down.

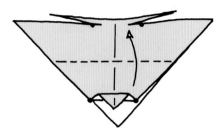

6 Fold up, joining the points.

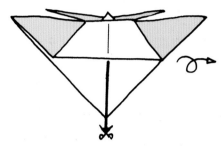

7 Cut on the heavy line, then turn it over.

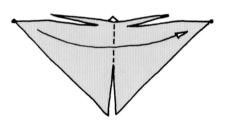

8 Fold in half.

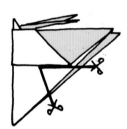

9 Cut through all the layers along the heavy lines.

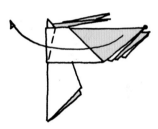

10 Fold the top wing on an angle …

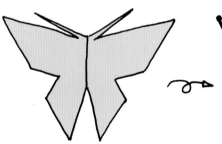

11 … like this, then turn over.

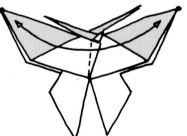

12 Fold the other wing, joining the points.

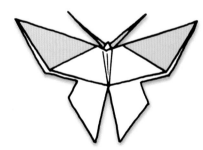

13 Open your butterfly and pull the antennae up.

Flower

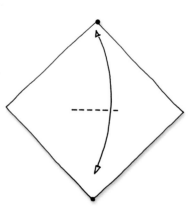

1 Fold a square of paper in half, marking only the center, then unfold.

▶ Beginner

Pick papers of all colors and create a magnificent garden or a beautiful bouquet.

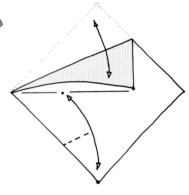

2 Fold the sides along the center crease, marking just the edges.

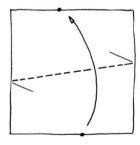

3 Fold up, connecting the edge marks.

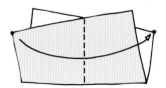

4 Fold in half, connecting the points.

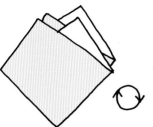

5 Rotate the model.

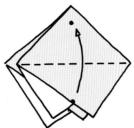

6 Fold up two layers …

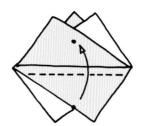

7 … then the other two layers …

8 … like this, then turn over.

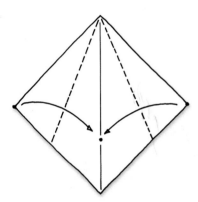

9 Fold the sides upward.

Enlarged View

10 Cut the lower point for the stem.

The Stem

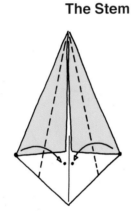

1 Fold the edges along the center crease, leaving a space between.

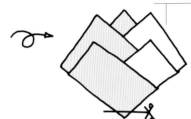

2 Fold the new edges along the center crease.

3 Fold the short sides as before.

4 Fold up the bottom, joining the points.

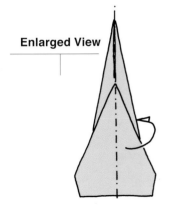

Enlarged View

5 Fold in half behind.

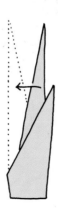

6 Separate the stems, flattening the model.

7 Put a flower on each stem.

43

Pine Tree

▶ Beginner

These pine trees are magnificent. If you create a forest, you can decorate the whole house. Hang them up or set them on a table for a lovely effect.

The Trunk and Branches

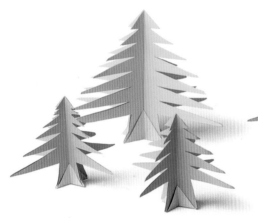

1 Fold a waterbomb base (see p. 12) from a square sheet of paper.

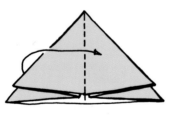

2 Fold everything in half.

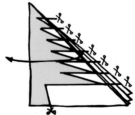

3 To create the branches, cut longer and longer notches, leaving space for the trunk. Open up to get two sets of branches on each side.

4 You can stop here and glue the parts of the trunk together. Or continue and make the base of the tree.

The Base

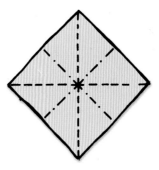

1 Fold a preliminary base (see p. 11) with a square one-third the size used for the trunk, then unfold.

2 Make creases by folding the four corners to the center, then refold the preliminary base.

Assembly

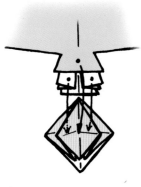

1 Place the trunk between the layers of the base as far as the crease.

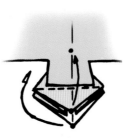

2 Fold up the triangles in front and back.

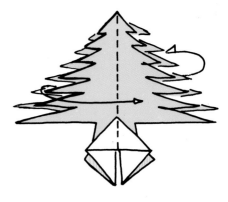

3 Fold one layer in front to the right and one in back to the left, and fold up the remaining triangles.

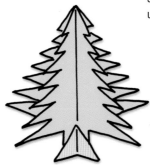

4 You can make trees of different sizes.

Ready for Takeoff

▶ Beginner

The large wings on this model give it a slow and stable flight. It is remarkably simple to fold.

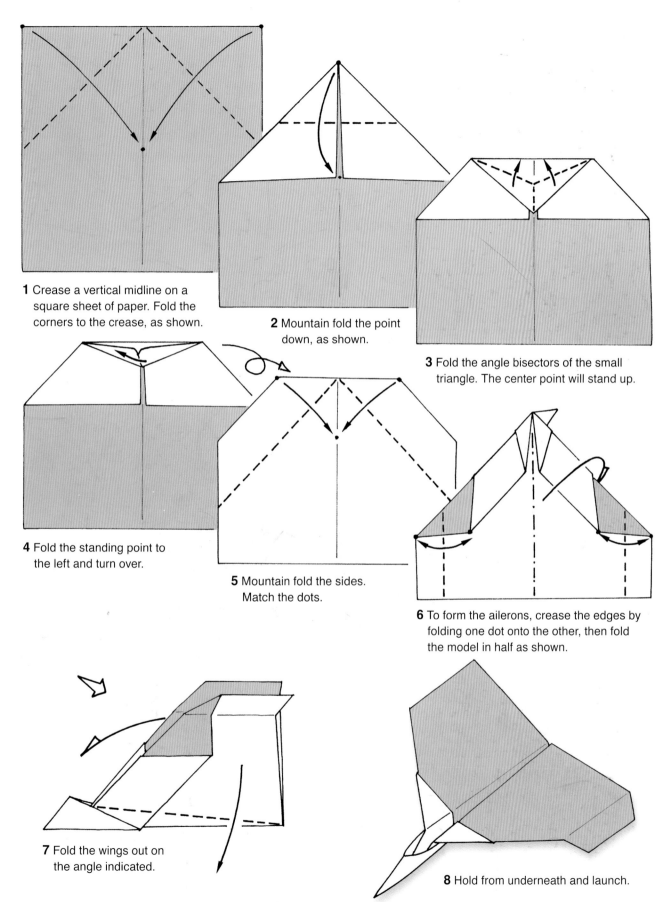

1 Crease a vertical midline on a square sheet of paper. Fold the corners to the crease, as shown.

2 Mountain fold the point down, as shown.

3 Fold the angle bisectors of the small triangle. The center point will stand up.

4 Fold the standing point to the left and turn over.

5 Mountain fold the sides. Match the dots.

6 To form the ailerons, crease the edges by folding one dot onto the other, then fold the model in half as shown.

7 Fold the wings out on the angle indicated.

8 Hold from underneath and launch.

Simple
Stars

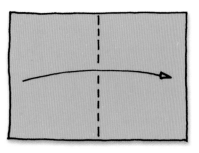

1 Fold a letter-sized, A4 or A5 sheet (see p. 16) in half.

▶ Beginner

A snip of the scissors, a few folds … and then, like magic, a galaxy of stars will appear in different sizes and styles.

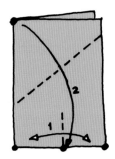

2 Mark the midpoint of the lower edge (1), then fold down the upper-left corner (2) to the middle of the side.

Enlarged View

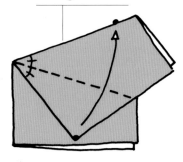

3 Fold the flap up along the upper edge.

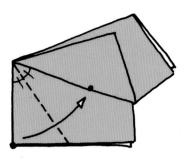

4 Fold the left side to the folded edge.

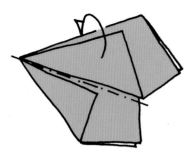

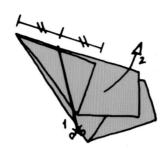

5 Fold in half toward the back.

6a Cut through all layers carefully (1), then unfold the point (2).

6b Give the star volume by making valley and mountain creases as shown.

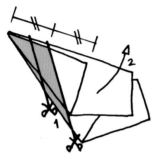

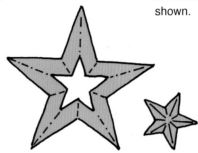

7a Cut along two parallel lines (1), then unfold the pieces (2).

7b You have a small star and a large one.

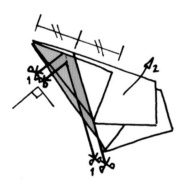

8a Cut as shown (1), taking note of the right angle, then unfold the small piece (2).

8b You have another type of star.

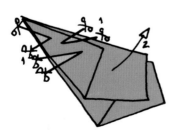

9a Cut out notches on the two sides (1), then unfold the sheet (2).

9b You have a star in the center of the sheet.

Delta Wing

The Delta Wing owes its originality to its nose and use of a clever locking technique. The variation on the original model is the asymmetry, which allows the model — if launched from a high place — to turn while flying.

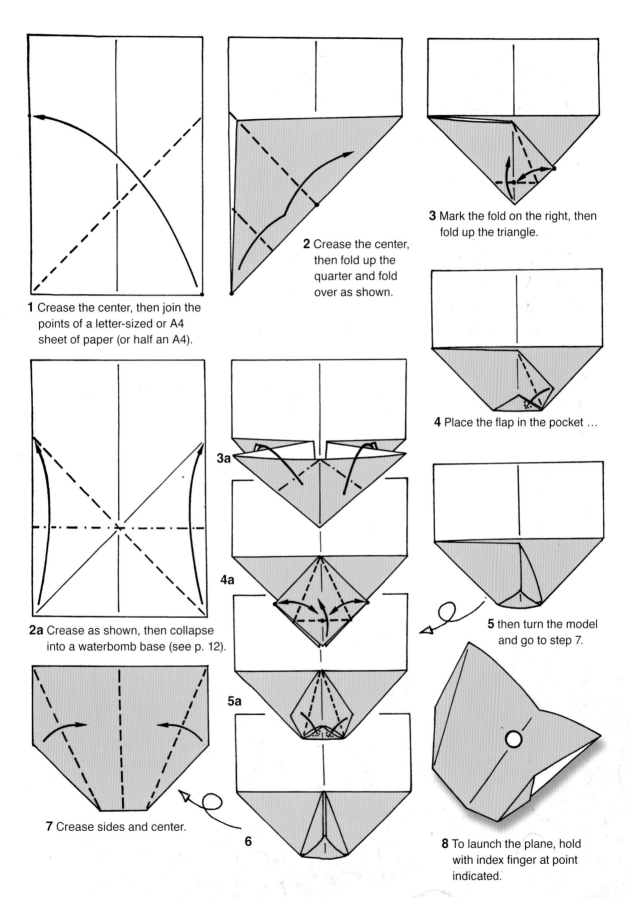

1 Crease the center, then join the points of a letter-sized or A4 sheet of paper (or half an A4).

2 Crease the center, then fold up the quarter and fold over as shown.

3 Mark the fold on the right, then fold up the triangle.

4 Place the flap in the pocket …

2a Crease as shown, then collapse into a waterbomb base (see p. 12).

3a

4a

5a

6

7 Crease sides and center.

5 then turn the model and go to step 7.

8 To launch the plane, hold with index finger at point indicated.

Mouth

▶ Beginner

Draw eyes and a nose on this character to amuse your friends. You can provide the voice as you move the mouth.

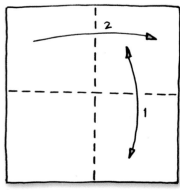

1 Crease the horizontal center of a square (1), then fold it in half to the right (2).

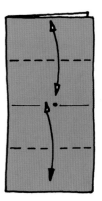

2 Crease by folding the ends to the center crease.

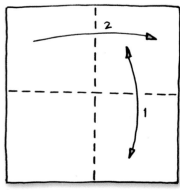

3 Fold the four corners, then unfold the corners on the right side.

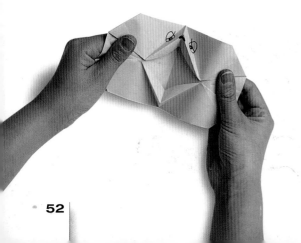

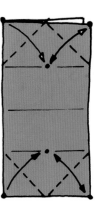

4 On the left side, fold the upper and lower corners back along the folded edge. On the right side, fold the top layer along the crease, then repeat behind.

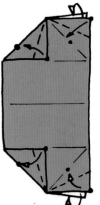

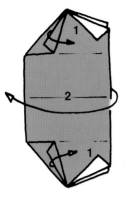

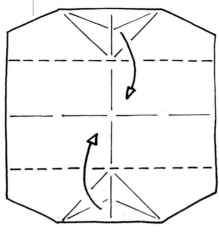

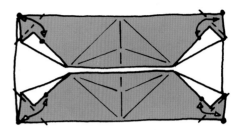

5 Unfold the corners on the left (1) and open up (2).

6 Refold the sides along the center crease.

7 Crease the four corners along the upper layer.

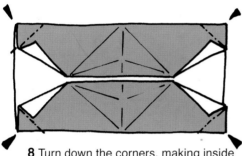

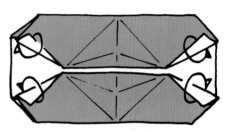

8 Turn down the corners, making inside reverse folds (see p. 13).

9 To lock the sides, reverse the flaps, folding them inside under all the layers.

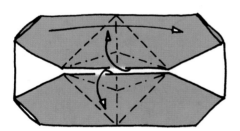

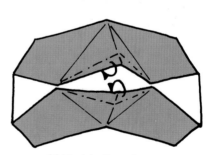

10 To shape the mouth, pull out the triangles as shown, then fold in half.

11 Tuck in the edges.

12 To make the mouth speak, hold the model at the points shown, then gently move your hands together and apart.

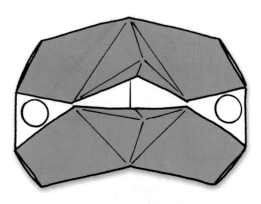

Hamster

These little rodents are an affectionate
and mischievous bunch.

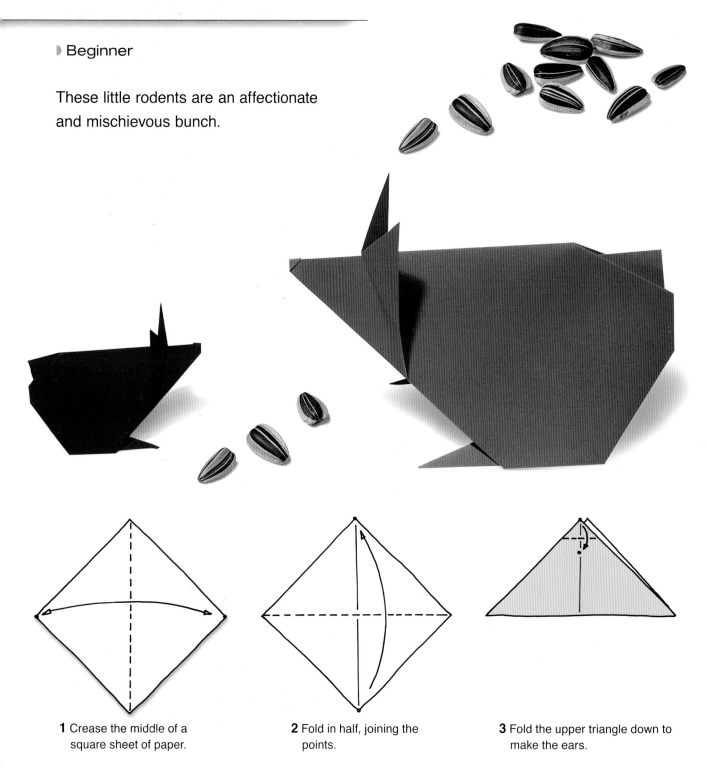

1 Crease the middle of a
square sheet of paper.

2 Fold in half, joining the
points.

3 Fold the upper triangle down to
make the ears.

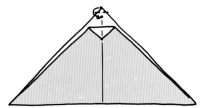

4 Fold another small triangle to form the nose …

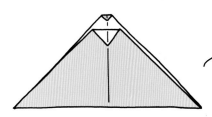

5 … like this, then turn it over.

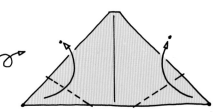

6 Fold the points toward the outside to make the feet.

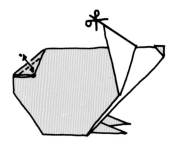

7 Narrow the feet by folding in half.

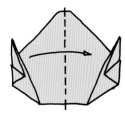

8 Fold everything in half.

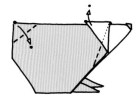

9 Pull up the ears, then flatten the new fold.

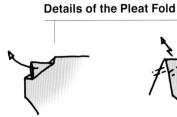

10 Separate the ears with a scissor cut. For the tail, make a pleat fold at the back.

Details of the Pleat Fold

11a Unfold.

11b Make an inside reverse fold (see p. 13) …

Details

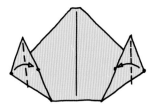

11c … open fold slightly …

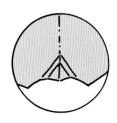

11d … then fold out the small triangle for the appearance of a tail.

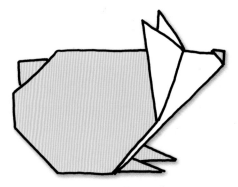

12 And you have a hamster.

Windblown

This model and its variation possess remarkable flight abilities. It will fly easily over a small or very large room.

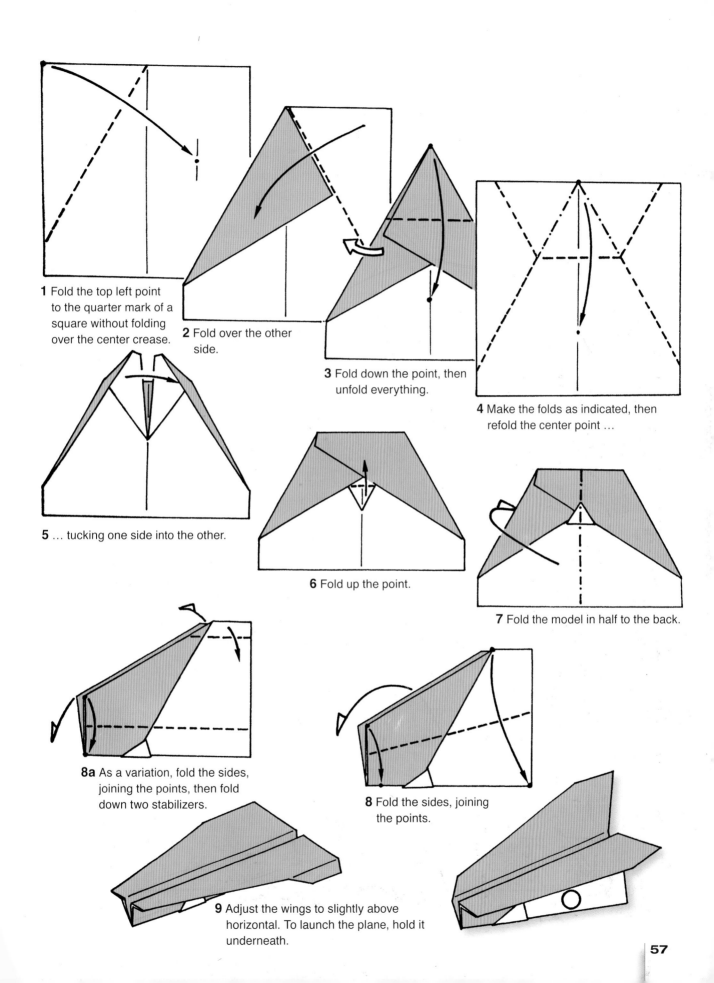

1 Fold the top left point to the quarter mark of a square without folding over the center crease.

2 Fold over the other side.

3 Fold down the point, then unfold everything.

4 Make the folds as indicated, then refold the center point …

5 … tucking one side into the other.

6 Fold up the point.

7 Fold the model in half to the back.

8a As a variation, fold the sides, joining the points, then fold down two stabilizers.

8 Fold the sides, joining the points.

9 Adjust the wings to slightly above horizontal. To launch the plane, hold it underneath.

Duck Plane

▶ Beginner

The origin of this airplane's name goes back to the beginnings of aviation. The "duck" was a plane that had its rudder in the front. It flew in 1907 with Louis Blériot at the controls. This paper version is a very capable flier.

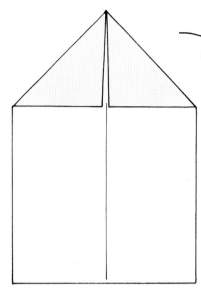

1 Crease lengthwise the center of a letter-sized or A4 sheet of paper. Fold corners to the midline …

2 … like this, then turn over.

3 Fold the sides to the midline crease along the diagonal, and free the back.

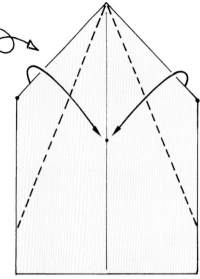

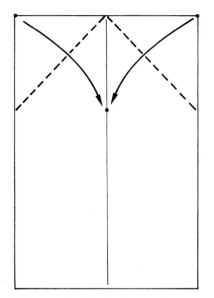

4 Mountain fold the top toward the back as shown.

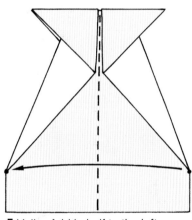

5 Valley fold in half to the left.

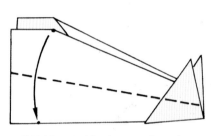

6 Fold one side down to the edge …

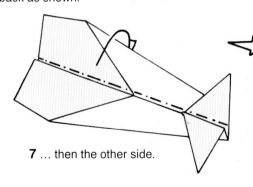

7 … then the other side.

8 Adjust the wings, and hold the plane from underneath to launch.

Seal

▶ Beginner

The seal has an inner sense of balance that makes it a natural at juggling balls. Seals usually live in cold polar waters, feeding on fish. At the end of the day when they are tired, they like to float on their sides.

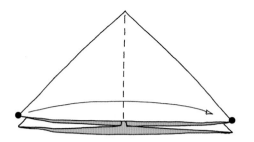

1 Start with a waterbomb base (see p. 12) with color inside. Fold one side to the right.

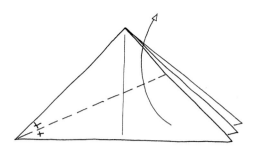

2 Fold the triangle up along the left edge bisecting the angle.

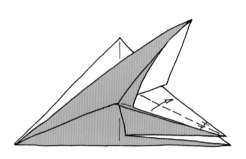

3 Then flatten the second layer to lie along the right-hand edge.

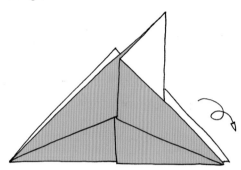

4 Like this, then turn over.

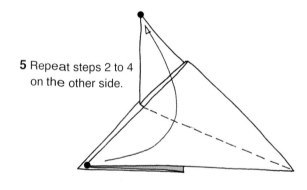

5 Repeat steps 2 to 4 on the other side.

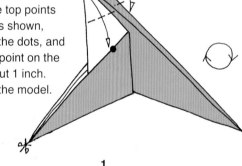

6 Fold the top points down as shown, joining the dots, and cut the point on the left about 1 inch. Rotate the model.

7 Fold the tips between the layers (1), then fold the upper point to the right for the head (2).

Head Details

7b Completely unfold the point.

7c Fold the tip over to create the nose (1). Cut the sides to form the whiskers (2), then refold the head on the folds as indicated.

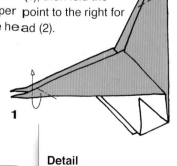

Detail

7a Detail of the tail.

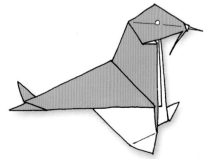

Bracelet

▶ Beginner

Decorate these beautiful colored bracelets to suit your taste or give them to your friends. If you use longer and wider strips, you can make a headband or decorative belt.

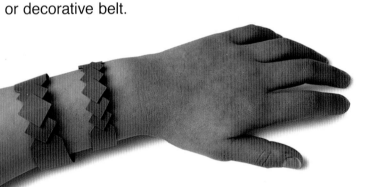

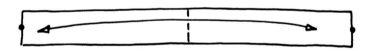

2 Crease the middle.

1 Cut a strip of paper from a letter-sized or A4 sheet (see p. 16). For a bracelet with three motifs, cut a strip 1 inch wide; for a bracelet with five motifs, cut a strip ⅝ inch wide.

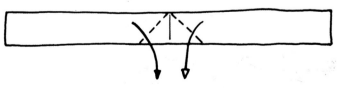

3 Fold the strip down along the center crease on both sides.

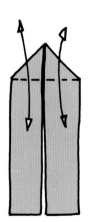

4 Make the horizontal crease by folding up both ends of the strip.

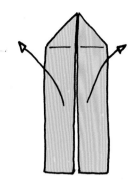

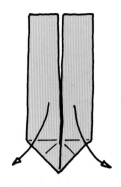

5 Unfold the strip.

6 Fold the strip up along the center crease on each side.

7 Unfold the strip.

Enlarged View

8 Refold along the creases …

9 … by joining the points.

10 Flatten, then fold the four corners.

11 Repeat steps 3 to 10 on each side of the central pattern.

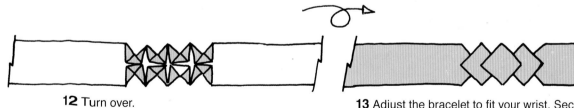

12 Turn over.

13 Adjust the bracelet to fit your wrist. Secure the ends with a drop of glue or a piece of double-sided tape.

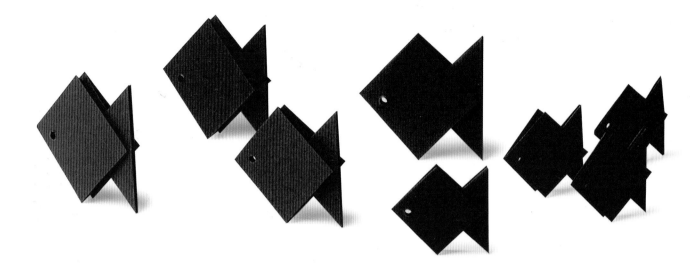

Fish

▶ Beginner

Fish like company, so they often travel in a school.

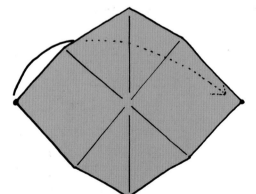

The Body

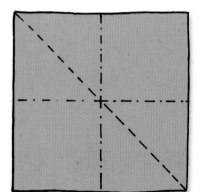

1 Use a square sheet with the colored side up. Mountain crease the horizontal and vertical, and valley crease one diagonal.

2 Fold the model, joining the points.

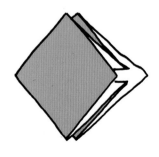

3 The body is finished.

The Tail

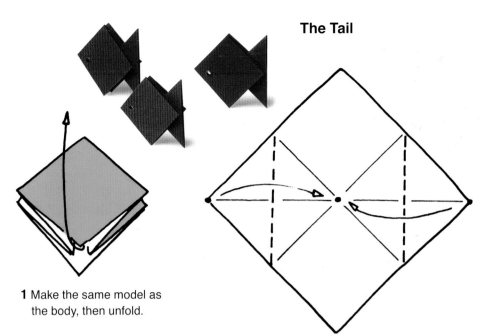

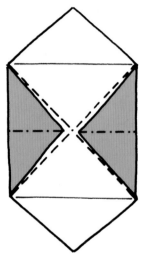

1 Make the same model as the body, then unfold.

2 Fold two corners to the center.

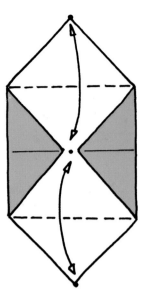

3 Fold and unfold the other two corners to the center.

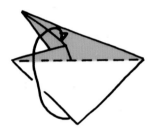

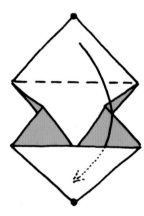

4 Refold the unit as in step 1, bringing in the two triangles.

5 Fold the rear triangle inside to lock the layers.

6 Fold the front triangle inside, the same way.

Assembly

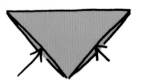

7 The unit has two pockets for assembly.

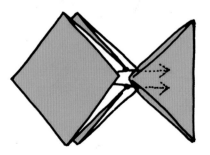

1 Slide the inside points of the body into the pockets of the tail.

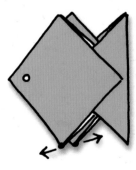

2 For the fish to stand, gently separate the points. Draw an eye with a pencil or punch a hole in the paper.

Chicks

▶ Beginner

What came first, the chicken or the egg? A riddle as
old as the world, which you can ponder while folding
a chick that's just been hatched from its shell.

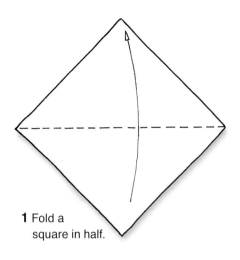

1 Fold a square in half.

2 Fold in half to the right.

3 Fold the upper point down to the left

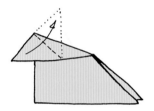

4 Fold the point back up.

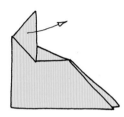

5 Unfold the point.

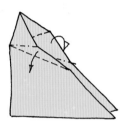

6 Refold using existing creases, opening the paper to the outside.

Head Detail

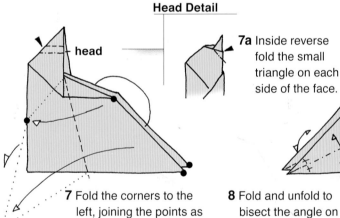

7a Inside reverse fold the small triangle on each side of the face.

7 Fold the corners to the left, joining the points as indicated. Repeat on the other side. Crimp fold the tip to form the beak (see p. 15).

8 Fold and unfold to bisect the angle on the left. Repeat on the other side. Reverse fold on these creases.

9 After prefolding (1), fold the points between the thicknesses (2) to fall in the same place.

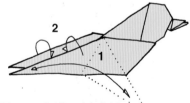

Back Details

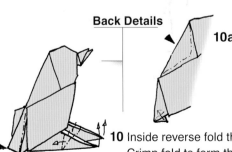

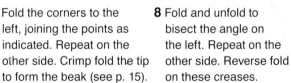

10a Fold the small triangle inside to lock in the back and push in to shape the back.

10 Inside reverse fold the back. Crimp fold to form the feet.

Sheep

▶▶ Intermediate

Sheep are very gentle animals with a thick coat of wool.
They bleat as they play, jumping in the air. The work of
a flock of sheep is to mow a meadow in record time,
without ever lifting up their heads from their jobs.

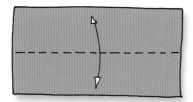

1 Crease the center line of a rectangle 1 x 2 (a half-square) color side up.

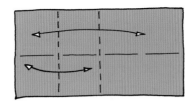

2 Crease the half and then the quarter.

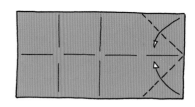

3 Fold the corners to the center crease, then turn over.

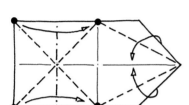

4 Crease the diagonals on the left side to make a waterbomb base (see p. 12). On the right side, fold as indicated bringing around the paper from behind.

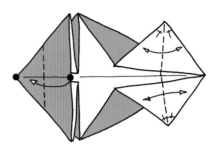

5 Open the left side by joining the dots; on the right side, crease to divide the angles in half.

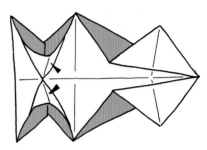

6 Flatten the left side.

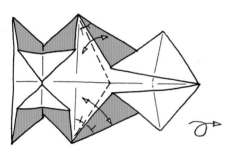

7 Mark the creases that divide the indicated angles and turn over.

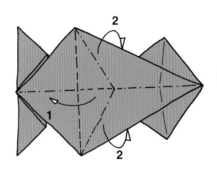

8 Valley fold on the vertical crease while mountain folding the diagonal creases (1). This will collapse the small triangle. Mountain fold along the central crease (2). These folds occur as one movement.

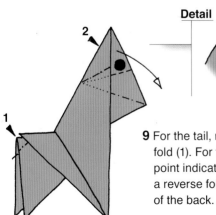

Detail

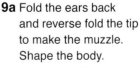

9a Fold the ears back and reverse fold the tip to make the muzzle. Shape the body.

9 For the tail, make a reverse fold (1). For the head, hold the point indicated (2) and make a reverse fold along the axis of the back.

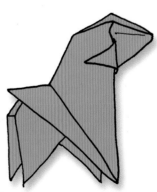

69

Garland

Intermediate

You can decorate the house for the holidays with these multicolored garlands. Make lots of small ones and string them together like pearls on a length of strong thread.

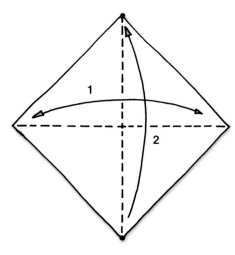

1 Crease a square sheet vertically (1), then fold up in half (2).

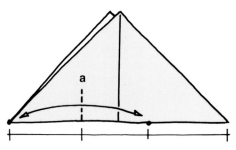

2 To divide perfectly in thirds, crease approximately one-third (a).

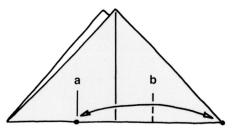

3 Make a second crease (b) by joining the points.

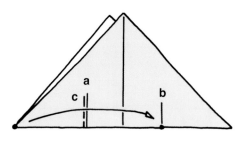

4 Make a third crease (c) by joining the points.

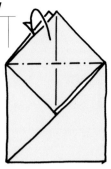

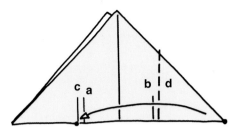

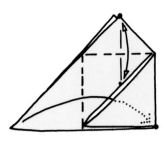

5 Finally, fold the right point to join (c).

6 Fold the other side inside the first, then crease the upper triangle through one layer.

7 Open the top slightly and tuck the upper triangle inside.

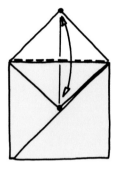

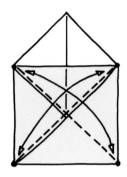

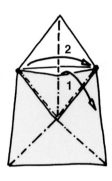

8 Crease the other triangle.

9 Crease the diagonals with a mountain crease and a valley crease.

10 Open the shape by pinching the small (1) and large triangles (2).

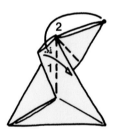

12 Make a set of small units in several colors, then …

11 To close the model, fold the small triangle (1) to the side, then tuck the point of the large triangle (2) inside the small one.

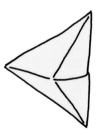

13 … using thread and a long needle, string the units together one by one, alternating colors.

Frisbee

A frisbee needs two people to play so both players should get involved in constructing the eight elements that make up this paper frisbee. Because it is a very light model, it can only be used indoors.

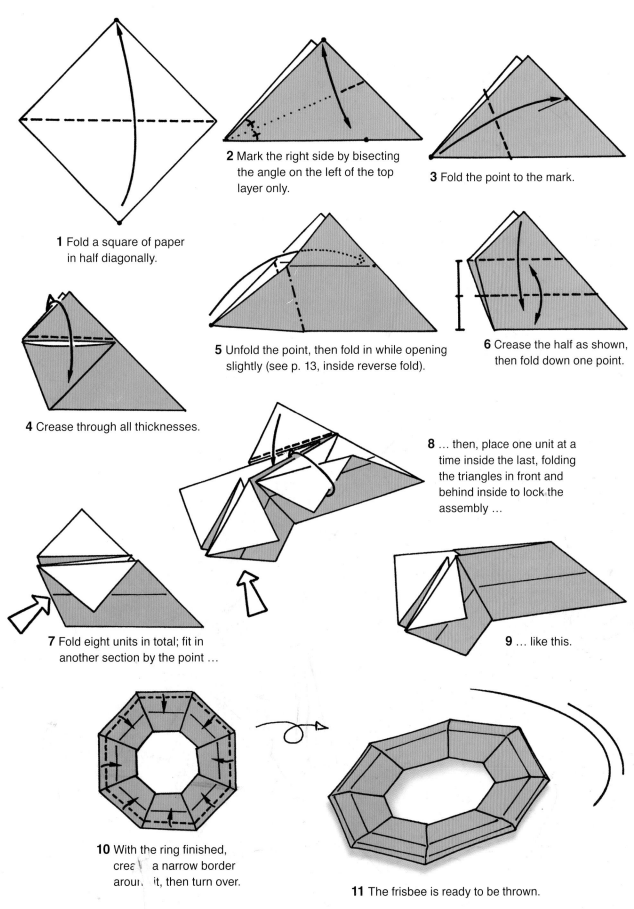

1 Fold a square of paper in half diagonally.

2 Mark the right side by bisecting the angle on the left of the top layer only.

3 Fold the point to the mark.

4 Crease through all thicknesses.

5 Unfold the point, then fold in while opening slightly (see p. 13, inside reverse fold).

6 Crease the half as shown, then fold down one point.

7 Fold eight units in total; fit in another section by the point …

8 … then, place one unit at a time inside the last, folding the triangles in front and behind inside to lock the assembly …

9 … like this.

10 With the ring finished, crea a narrow border arour it, then turn over.

11 The frisbee is ready to be thrown.

Looping

This model is made from a small square of paper. If you stretch out your arm when you throw it, it will delight you with a series of aerial acrobatics before landing a few yards away.

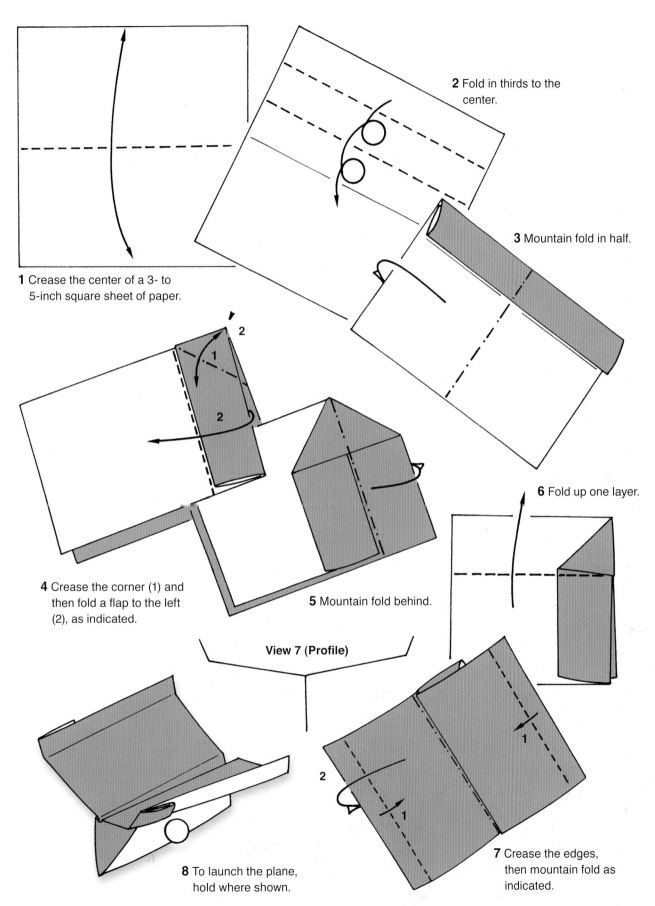

1 Crease the center of a 3- to 5-inch square sheet of paper.

2 Fold in thirds to the center.

3 Mountain fold in half.

4 Crease the corner (1) and then fold a flap to the left (2), as indicated.

5 Mountain fold behind.

6 Fold up one layer.

View 7 (Profile)

7 Crease the edges, then mountain fold as indicated.

8 To launch the plane, hold where shown.

Elephant

Elephants always live near a source of water for drinking and bathing. And they like to play in the water too, just like kids — making waves and splashing their playmates.

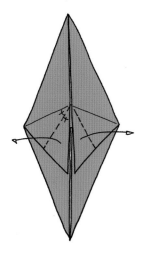
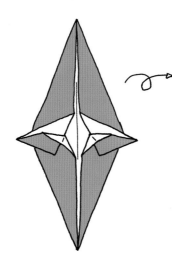
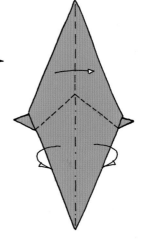
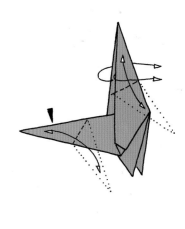

1 Start with the fish base (see p. 14). Bisect the angles as shown, folding the points to the outside.

2 While folding the points out, flatten the inner folds. Turn over.

3 Crease the diagonals, then fold in half on the long vertical.

4 Outside reverse fold the upper point after prefolding (see p. 13). Inside reverse fold the left-hand point after prefolding.

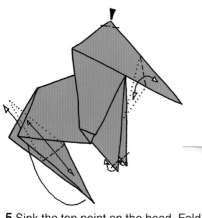

5 Sink the top point on the head. Fold and unfold trunk as shown. To form tail, inside reverse fold point on left. Outside reverse fold the front feet and spread the front legs.

Details

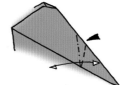

5a Crimp fold the trunk.

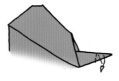

5b Squash fold the tip (see p. 12).

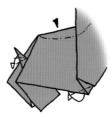

5c Fold in the points on the elephant's belly. Squash fold the tip of the tail and round the back. To finish, shape the ears.

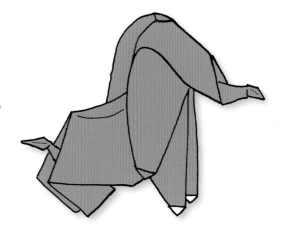

Dog

» Intermediate

This dog resembles a fox because of its square muzzle and pointed ears.

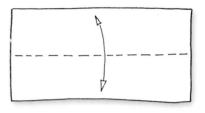

1 Mark the center fold of a rectangle 1 x 2 (a half-square).

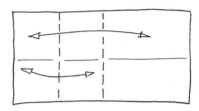

2 Mark the half, then the quarter.

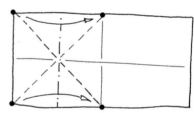

3 Fold the diagonals, then make a waterbomb base (see p. 12).

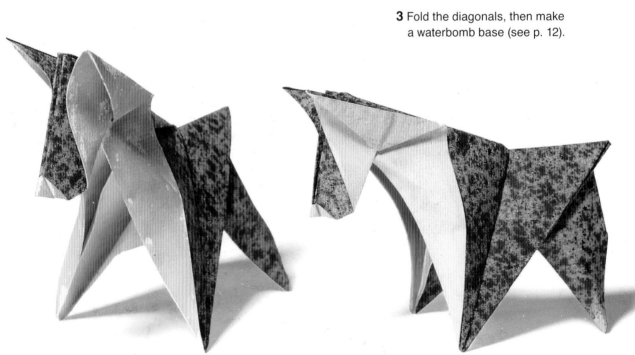

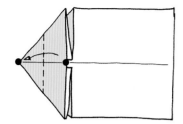

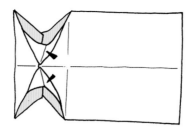

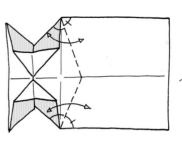

4 Open up by joining the points.

5 Flatten completely.

6 Precrease by dividing the angle in half, then turn over.

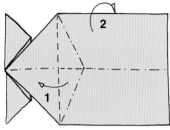

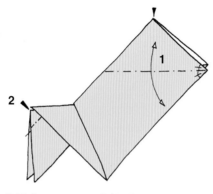

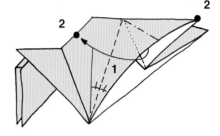

7 Valley fold on the vertical crease while mountain folding the diagonal creases (1). This will collapse the small triangle. Mountain fold along the central crease (2). These folds occur as one movement.

8 Make a reverse fold after precreasing the angle in half (1). Reverse fold the small corner (on the left) to indicate the tail (2).

9 Open and fold down the top thickness of paper to the vertical line (1). The model will naturally lie flat on joining the points (2). Repeat on the other side.

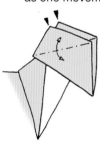

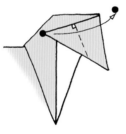

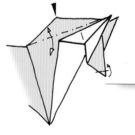

Neck Details

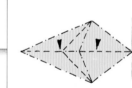

10 Make a reverse fold after precreasing for the ears.

11 Fold a right angle as shown and press the point of the ear flat. Repeat on the other ear.

12 For the nose, fold back the point and open slightly. On the top, make a precrease before sinking the point as shown.

12a Find the indicated creases and push inside. If this is too difficult, simply fold the triangle of the neck back to the previous step.

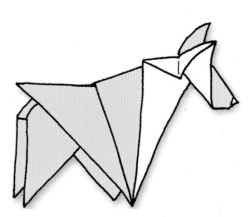

Silent Spinner

This propeller is a modified traditional model. These three strips woven together will come alive with a rustling of paper when you put them on the tip of a pencil and whirl it around.

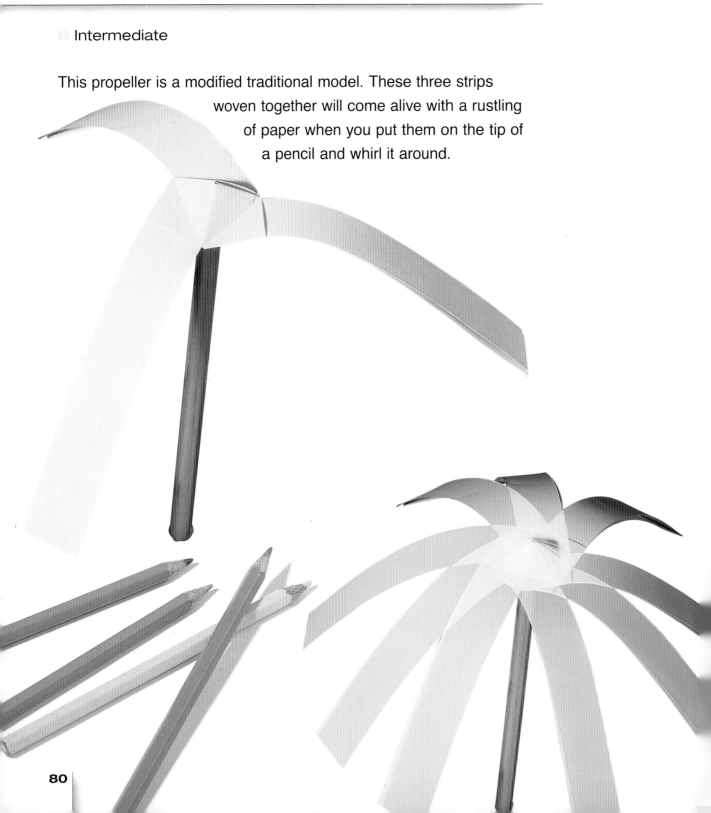

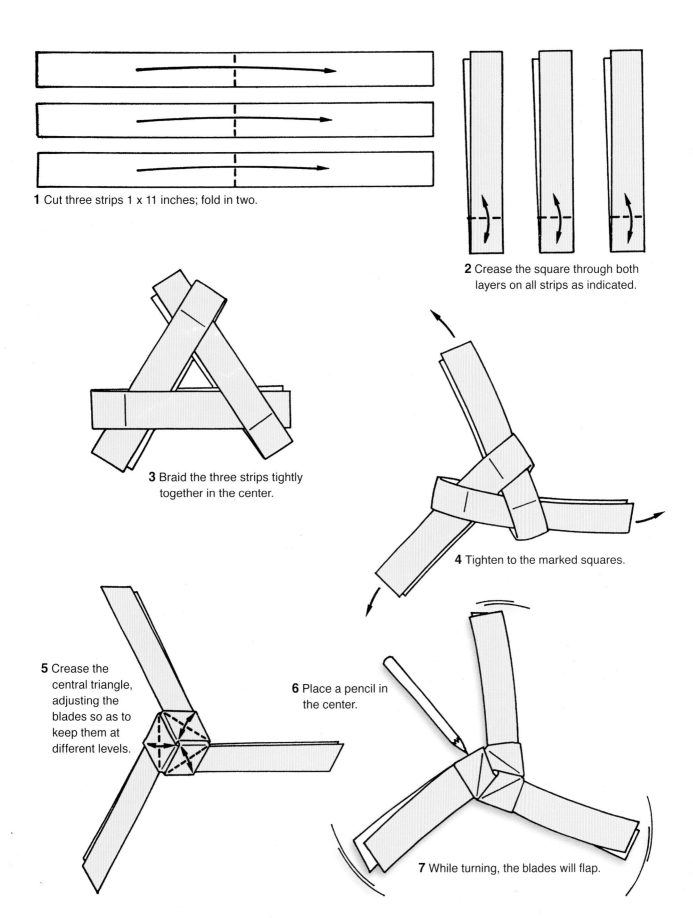

1 Cut three strips 1 x 11 inches; fold in two.

2 Crease the square through both layers on all strips as indicated.

3 Braid the three strips tightly together in the center.

4 Tighten to the marked squares.

5 Crease the central triangle, adjusting the blades so as to keep them at different levels.

6 Place a pencil in the center.

7 While turning, the blades will flap.

Propeller

▶▶ Intermediate

Philip Shen created the propeller on which this model is based. You'll find the model extremely simple to make. You may pin it to a dowel or a piece of wood, tacking the head down from the inside in the center of the propeller. When you move the dowel, the propeller will turn with the whir of a motor.

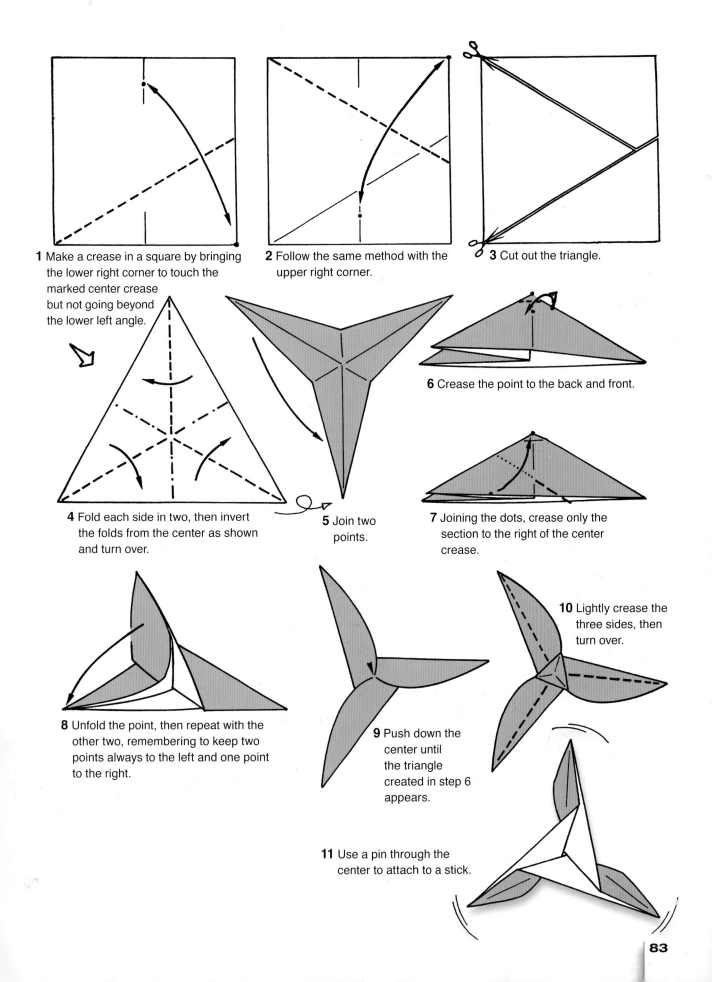

1 Make a crease in a square by bringing the lower right corner to touch the marked center crease but not going beyond the lower left angle.

2 Follow the same method with the upper right corner.

3 Cut out the triangle.

4 Fold each side in two, then invert the folds from the center as shown and turn over.

5 Join two points.

6 Crease the point to the back and front.

7 Joining the dots, crease only the section to the right of the center crease.

8 Unfold the point, then repeat with the other two, remembering to keep two points always to the left and one point to the right.

9 Push down the center until the triangle created in step 6 appears.

10 Lightly crease the three sides, then turn over.

11 Use a pin through the center to attach to a stick.

Rabbit

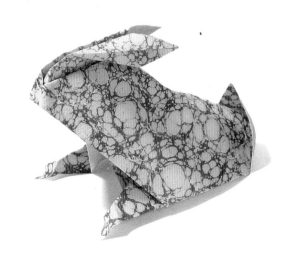

▶▶ Intermediate

In the wild, rabbits live in family groups deep under the earth in burrows they have dug themselves. Its acute hearing, thanks to big ears, alerts it to danger. This rabbit is a little more detailed than the one on page 22.

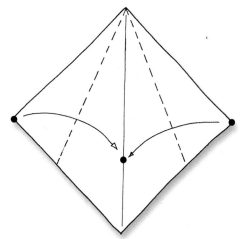

1 Fold the sides of a square to the center crease.

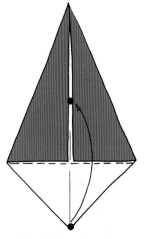

2 Fold the triangle up.

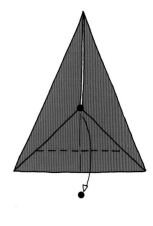

3 Fold the tip back down, joining the points.

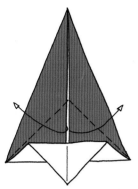

4 Pull out the corners, folding them along the edge of the preceding fold.

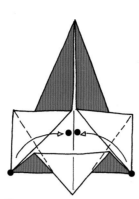

5 Fold in the sides as shown.

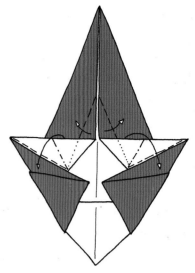

6 To narrow the points, fold down one layer and open along marked folds.

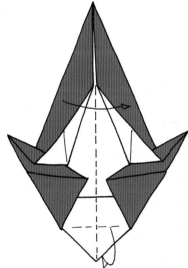

7 Bend the bottom point to the back to make the tail, then fold model in half along the vertical.

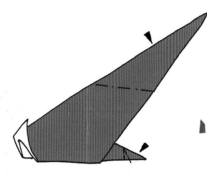

8 After precreasing, reverse fold the large point. For the feet, make squash folds as for the ears (steps 11 and 12). Loosen the tail and shape the body.

Head Detail

9 Inside reverse fold (see p. 13).

Ear Details

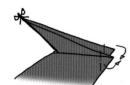

10 Cut the point in two to separate the ears. Fold the tips at the front inside, sliding one inside the other to form the muzzle.

11 Squash fold (see p. 12).

12 Like this. Shape the ears, then the back, to give your rabbit volume.

Mouse

)) Intermediate

When the cat's away, the mice will play. They're
especially fond of playing on attic floors while
they nibble grain.

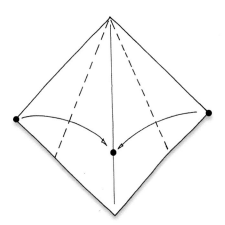

1 Fold the sides of a square to the center crease.

2 Like this, then turn over.

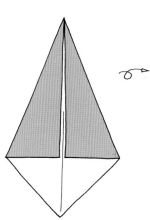

3 Fold as shown, joining the dots.

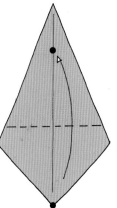

4 Fold the sides flat.

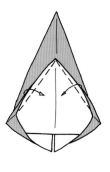

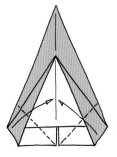

5 Fold the sides up along the center crease.

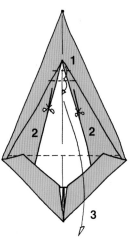

6 Fold down the point twice (1), cut thin strips as indicated for whiskers (2), and fold the upper point toward the bottom (3).

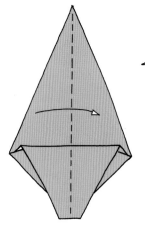

7 Fold in two along vertical fold.

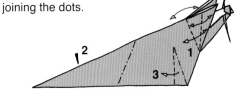

8 Precrease the ears as shown (1). Fold out the whiskers. Make an inside reverse fold (see p. 13) for the tail (2). Crimp fold to create volume: this fold can slip between two layers on the inside (3).

Ear Details

8a Squash fold (see p. 12).

8b Fold in two.

8c Open slightly on one side.

8d Like this.

Tail Details

9b Curve the tail.

9a Narrow the tail by folding the edges inside.

9 Bring up the point with an inside reverse fold (see p. 13) and open the sides slightly.

To make a standing mouse, fold the tail quite high in step 9 and narrow it as in step 9a.

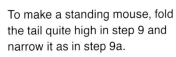

87

Box and House

Only a tiny person could live in this delightful little house. But with just two folds and a spin, the house becomes a box … perfect for candy.

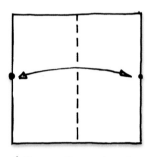

1 Crease the center of a square.

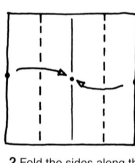

2 Fold the sides along the center crease …

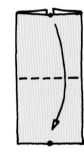

3 … like this, then turn it over.

4 Fold in half.

Enlarged View

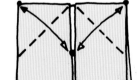

5 Crease the corners by joining the points.

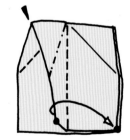

6 To make the corner a reverse fold, fold one layer to the right, pushing in the corner …

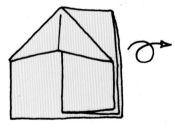

7 … like this, then turn it over.

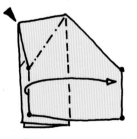

8 Fold the other corner the same way.

88

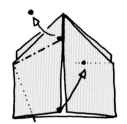

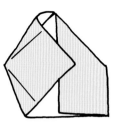

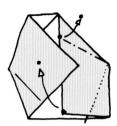

9 Flip the upper layer in front to the left and the rear one to the right.

10 Bring the lower corner up to the dotted horizontal line …

11 … then flatten.

12 Repeat steps 10 and 11 on the other corner …

Enlarged View

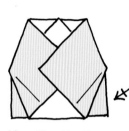

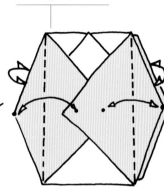

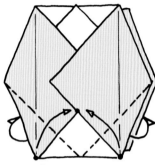

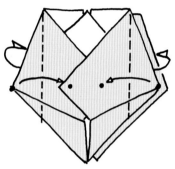

13 … like this. Repeat the steps on the two corners on the other side.

14 Crease the sides front and back.

15 Fold up the lower triangles by joining the points. Repeat behind.

16 Refold the sides. Repeat behind.

The House

The Box

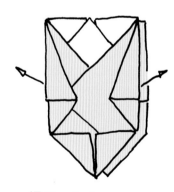

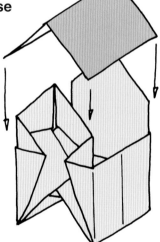

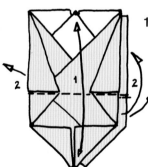

19 After step 16, crease as shown on both sides (1), then give the box volume by putting your fingers inside (2).

17 Give the house volume by placing your fingers inside and sharpening the creases.

18 To make the roof, simply fold a small square or rectangle in half.

20 To make nesting boxes (boxes that fit inside one another), just fold them from slightly smaller squares.

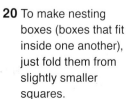

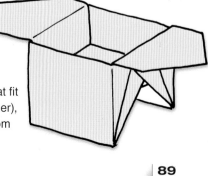

String of Dolls

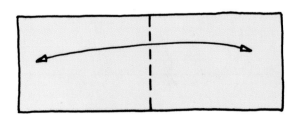

▶▶ Intermediate

Make some simple folds and scissor cuts, and you have a string of little dancing people. To make a circle, join several strings together.

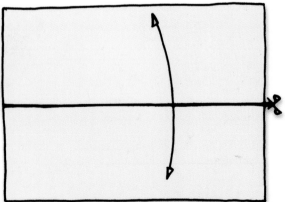

1 Fold a letter-sized or A4 sheet in half, then cut along the crease.

2 Crease the center.

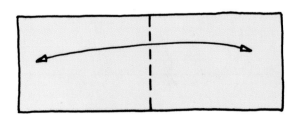

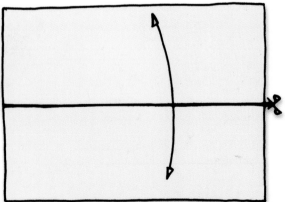

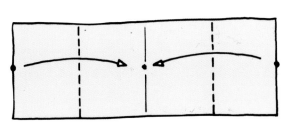

3 Fold the edges along the center crease …

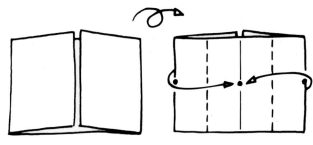

4 … like this, then turn it over.

5 Fold the sides to the center crease, freeing the layers behind.

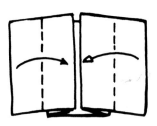

6 Fold in the remaining strips the same way.

Enlarged View

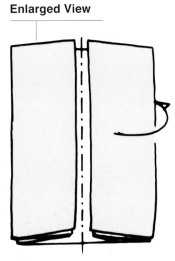

7 Fold in half behind.

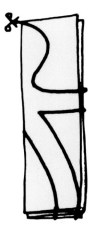

8 With a pencil, draw the silhouette of a person, then cut through all layers.

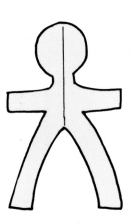

9 Unfold completely to show the string.

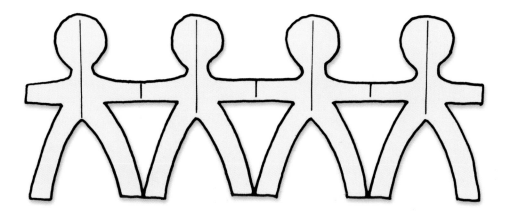

10 To make a circle of dolls, make another string with the leftover half and glue the ends together.

Windmill

▶ Intermediate

Thrown from a certain height, this model will turn at an ever-increasing speed because its bent blades scoop up air during the fall. You can also place it on a thin wire or thread and it will twirl as the wind blows.

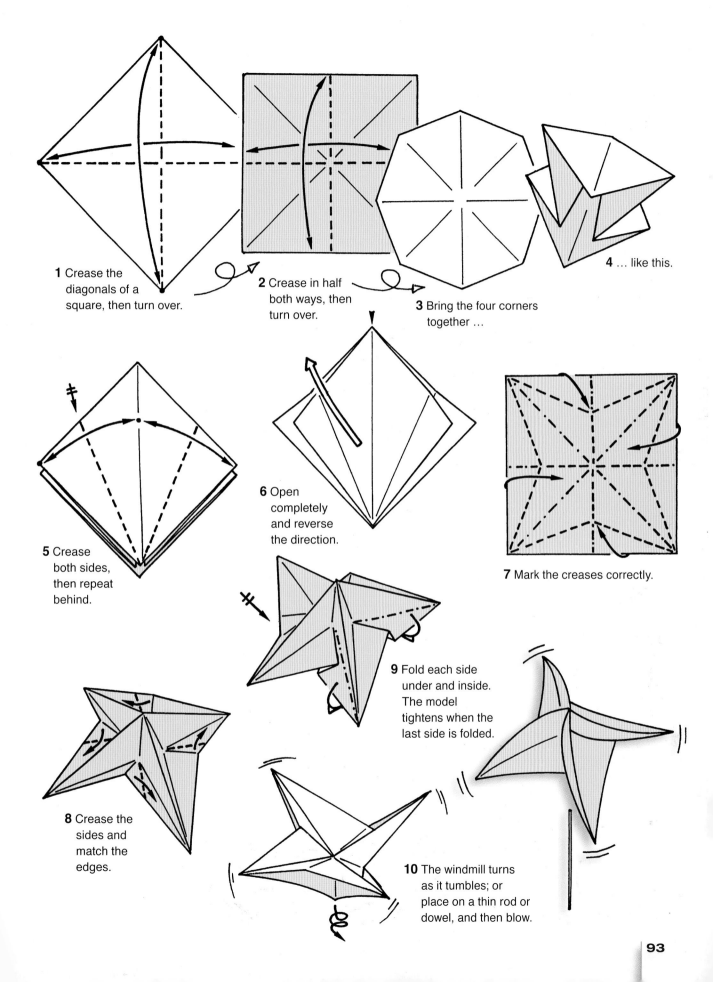

1 Crease the diagonals of a square, then turn over.

2 Crease in half both ways, then turn over.

3 Bring the four corners together …

4 … like this.

5 Crease both sides, then repeat behind.

6 Open completely and reverse the direction.

7 Mark the creases correctly.

8 Crease the sides and match the edges.

9 Fold each side under and inside. The model tightens when the last side is folded.

10 The windmill turns as it tumbles; or place on a thin rod or dowel, and then blow.

Imaginary
Voyage

In our dreams, we often fly over imaginary lands. This little
airplane will allow us to travel in spirit as if in a fairy tale.

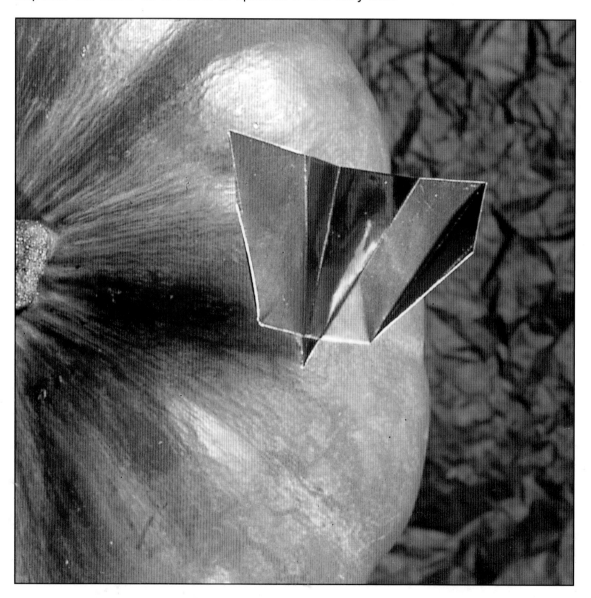

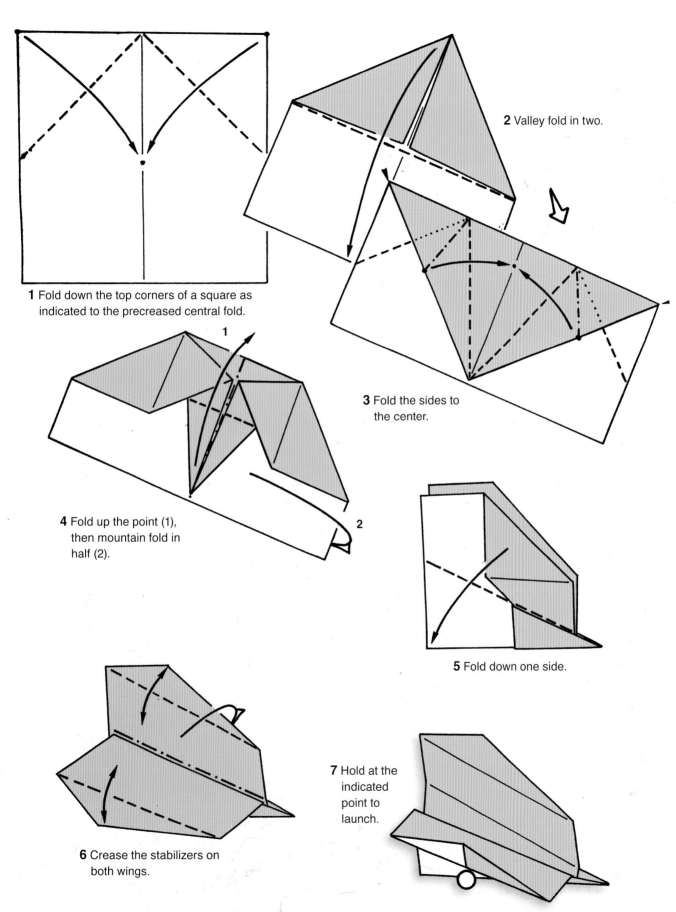

1 Fold down the top corners of a square as indicated to the precreased central fold.

2 Valley fold in two.

3 Fold the sides to the center.

4 Fold up the point (1), then mountain fold in half (2).

5 Fold down one side.

6 Crease the stabilizers on both wings.

7 Hold at the indicated point to launch.

Turtle

▶▶ Intermediate

Turtles can grow up to 8 feet and can weigh up to 650 pounds. More at home in water than on land, turtles swim well because of their long, flattened, fin-like feet. What is most admired is the beauty of the carapace, which varies in color and pattern from one species to another. Now it's up to you to decorate your turtle. Let your imagination go wild.

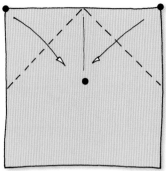

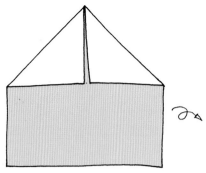

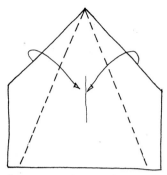

1 Starting with a square, color side up, crease the center vertically as shown. Fold the corners down along this crease, joining the dots.

2 Like this, then turn over.

3 Fold the edges to the center crease, allowing the corners from behind to flip to the front.

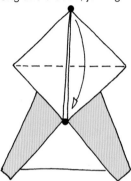

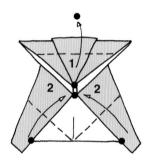

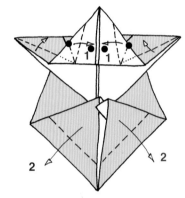

4 Fold the square in half.

5 Fold up a third by joining the points (1), then fold the bottom edges along the vertical axis (2).

6 To form the front legs, join the points noting the fold lines (1) while narrowing the head. Then fold back the back legs (2).

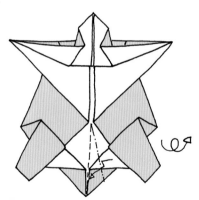

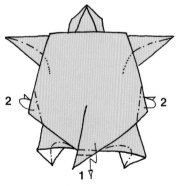

7 Add volume to the shell with a crimp fold, then turn over.

8 Make a pleat fold in the tail to lock in the back fold (1), then shape the legs and the head. To round the shell, fold under the corners on the sides (2).

Swimming Fish

Intermediate

The fish rest on three supporting points, giving the illusion that they are swimming in the water, drifting along with the current. It's up to you to create a lively school of fish in movement.

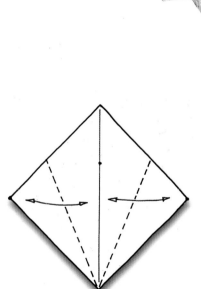

1 After creasing the diagonal of a square, fold and unfold the lower edge to the center crease.

2 Fold the upper edges in the same way.

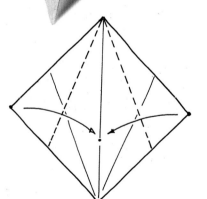

3 Fold the corners up using the creases from step 1 and the new mountain fold indicated.

4 Cut along the bold line and fold the model in two to the rear.

5 Fold one point down vertically.

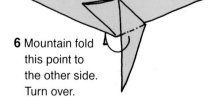

6 Mountain fold this point to the other side. Turn over.

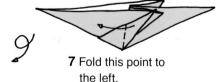

7 Fold this point to the left.

8 Then to the right.

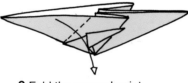

9 Fold the second point down vertically.

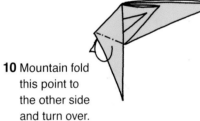

10 Mountain fold this point to the other side and turn over.

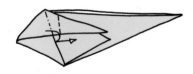

11 Pleat fold this point and lock between the two layers.

Tail Details

12a Unfold.

12b Reverse fold the point.

12c Cut this point in two.

12d Like this.

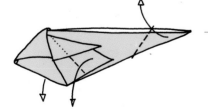

12 Fold down vertically the triangles on each side, then fold the point of the tail up to the vertical.

12e Fold the top point down.

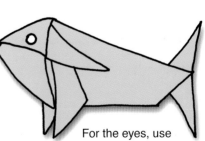

For the eyes, use a hole punch.

Pyramid

▶▶ Intermediate

The pyramids of Egypt were filled with rich treasures. These little pyramids can serve as money boxes or banks. Slide your money in along the edges; take it out by lifting the little pointed top.

The Base

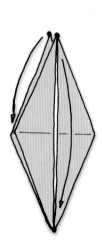

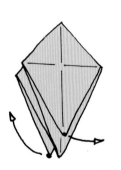

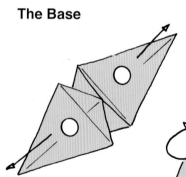

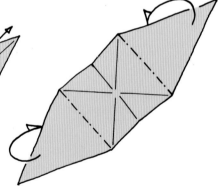

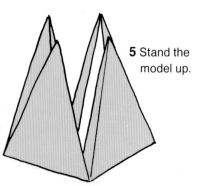

1 Start with a bird base (see p. 15), then fold the two points down.

2 Pull the two points out at the same time, halfway.

3 Hold the points shown, in both hands, then pull lightly to make the square bottom of the pyramid.

4 Join the four points.

5 Stand the model up.

The Top

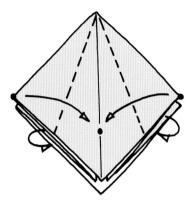

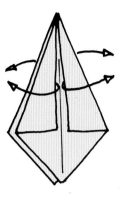

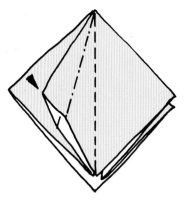

1 Start with a preliminary base (see p. 11) made with a smaller square, then fold the edges along the center crease on both faces.

2 Unfold the sides.

3 Raise one side to vertical, then open as you flatten it.

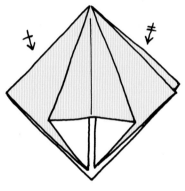

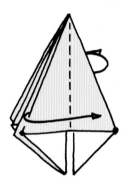

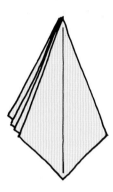

4 Repeat this step on the other three sides.

5 Fold the front layer to the right, then fold the back layer to the left.

6 Give it shape by making four faces.

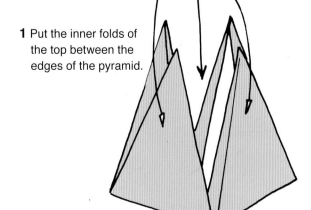

Assembly

1 Put the inner folds of the top between the edges of the pyramid.

2 You can change the size of the top by folding smaller or larger squares.

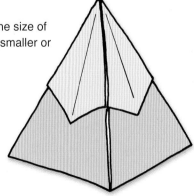

Face

▶▶ Intermediate

A pointed nose or a round one? Blue eyes or brown eyes? Mouth open or closed? It's your choice when you make these funny faces.

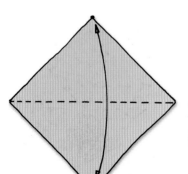

1 Crease a square in half.

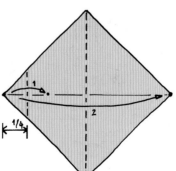

2 Fold in the corner one-quarter of the way (1), then fold in half (2).

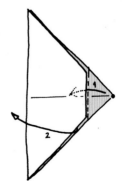

3 Fold the exposed corner to the inside to match the first corner folded (1), then open the model (2).

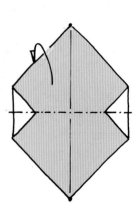

4 Fold in half behind.

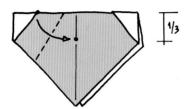

5 Fold the left corner in thirds, then join the points.

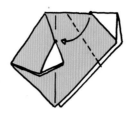

6 Fold the other corner the same way.

7 Bring up the right side as shown.

Enlarged View

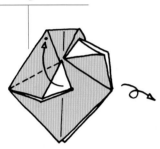

8 Fold up the left side, then turn over.

Enlarged View

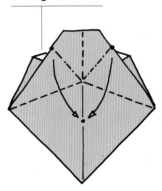

9 Fold down the sides along two corresponding valley folds on the other side and flatten.

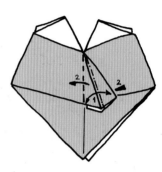

10 To give shape to the nose, crease along the upper layer (1), then spread open and flatten (2).

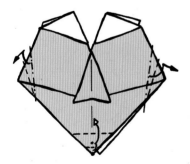

11 Make pleat folds for the ears. For the mouth, fold the point up, then fold again.

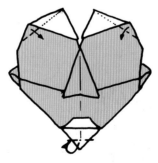

12 To finish the mouth, fold the point behind, then shape the eyes by folding forward, as shown.

13 Fold back the part behind the eyes.

Schoolboy

Although the folding technique of this airplane is very sophisticated, it shouldn't present any difficulties. The thickness of its nose makes this plane a good outdoor flyer.

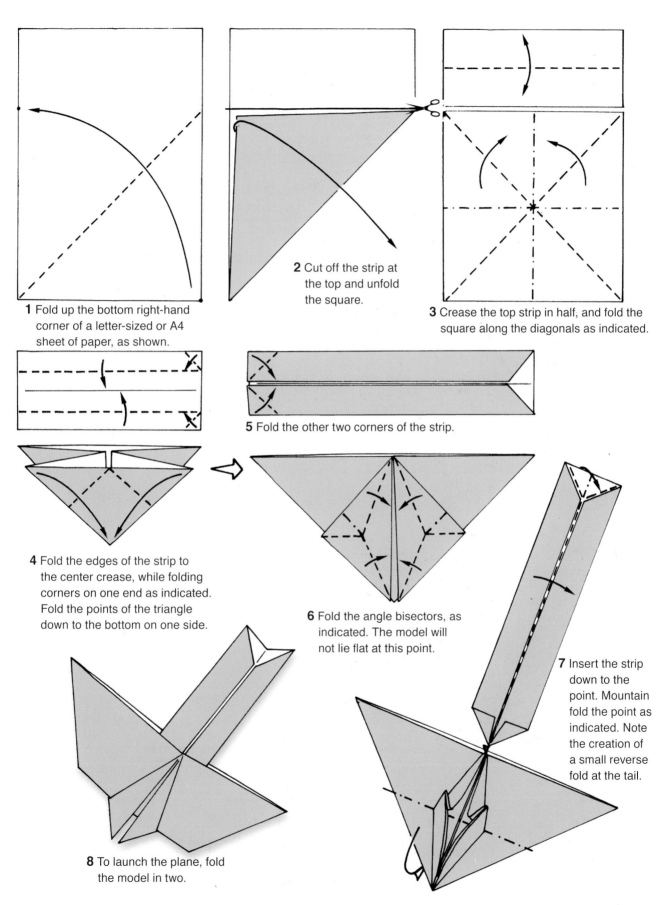

1 Fold up the bottom right-hand corner of a letter-sized or A4 sheet of paper, as shown.

2 Cut off the strip at the top and unfold the square.

3 Crease the top strip in half, and fold the square along the diagonals as indicated.

4 Fold the edges of the strip to the center crease, while folding corners on one end as indicated. Fold the points of the triangle down to the bottom on one side.

5 Fold the other two corners of the strip.

6 Fold the angle bisectors, as indicated. The model will not lie flat at this point.

7 Insert the strip down to the point. Mountain fold the point as indicated. Note the creation of a small reverse fold at the tail.

8 To launch the plane, fold the model in two.

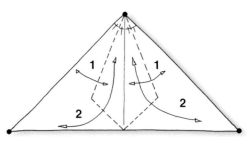

1 Starting with a half-square, precrease the edges to the vertical center fold (1), then crease the folds at the base by joining the end points to the apex (2).

Dove

⏵⏵ Intermediate

This white bird is often depicted in flight with an olive branch in its beak: a symbol of peace. You can suspend the dove by attaching nylon thread to each wing.

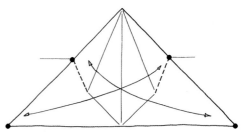

2 To make this crease, fold each point to the opposite edge making sure to keep the top edges horizontal.

2a Like this, then unfold.

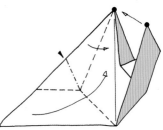

3 Make reverse folds as shown, joining the points and using the existing creases.

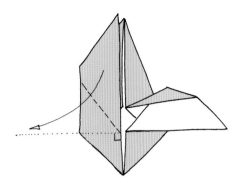

4 Valley fold back the points to lie on the horizontal and flatten the interior folds.

Back

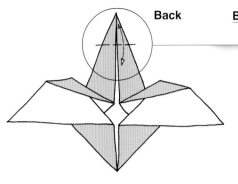

5 Fold and unfold the upper point, then open this point.

Back Details

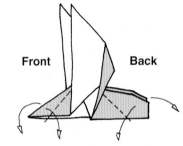

5a Fold the tip down using the existing creases, making the necessary valley to mountain fold adjustments, then close. Turn over.

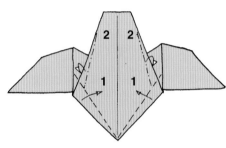

6 Valley fold the lower edges (1), then mountain fold the upper edges (2) to shape the body.

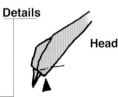

7 Fold in half.

Front   Back

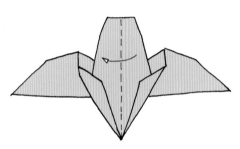

8 At both the front and back, make outside reverse folds (see p. 13).

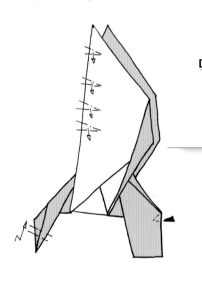

9 Crimp fold the point of the head to form the beak. To curve the wings, make a series of small crimp folds.

Details

Head

9a Inside reverse fold (see p. 13) the corners on each side.

Tail

9b Push in the center of an imaginary triangle as shown to create volume.

Dragonfly

▶▶ Intermediate

The dragonfly has four transparent wings as delicate as lace. In flight, the buzzing of the wings sounds like a helicopter's blades in the air. Sometimes dragonflies enjoy performing aerial acrobatics just above water level.

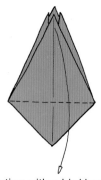

1 Starting with a bird base (see p. 15), fold one point down.

2 Fold the two points vertically, then open and flatten evenly (squash fold) as on the right.

3 Like this, then turn over.

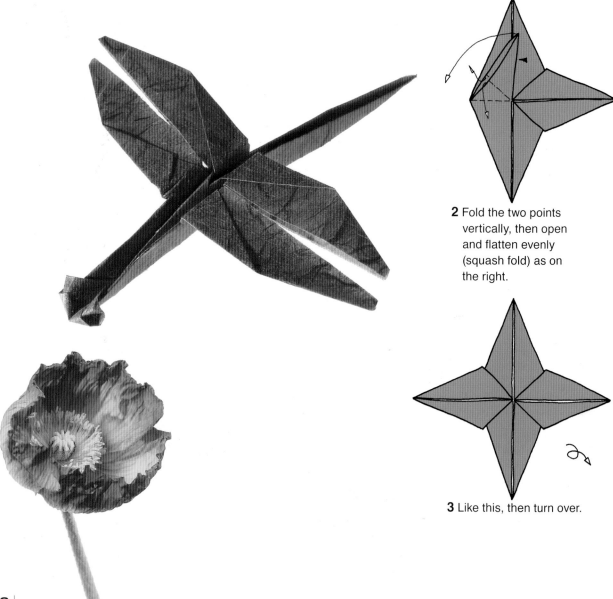

108

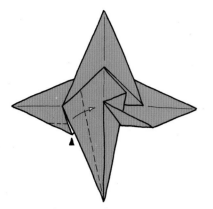

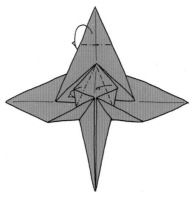

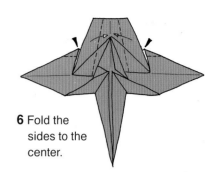

6 Fold the sides to the center.

4 Fold the sides to the center crease as on the right.

5 Fold back the upper point. Fold the inner corners: the left-hand corner folds under.

Detail

6a Fold and unfold the flaps, then unfold the sides.

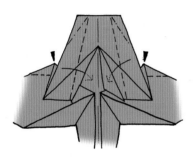

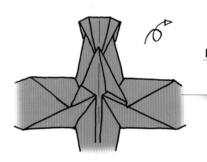

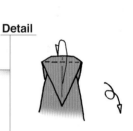

Detail

7 Refold the sides under the central triangle.

8 Like this, then turn over.

8a Fold the triangle up and over the top, sliding it under the other layers. Turn over.

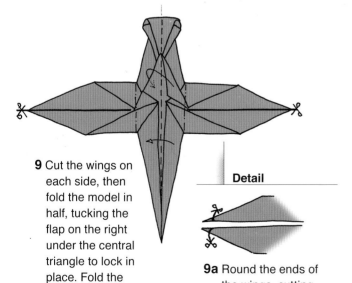

9 Cut the wings on each side, then fold the model in half, tucking the flap on the right under the central triangle to lock in place. Fold the wings down.

Detail

9a Round the ends of the wings, cutting with scissors.

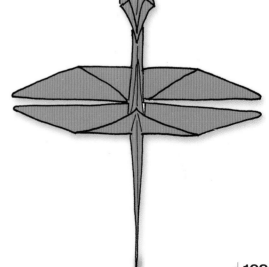

Grasshopper

The grasshopper, found in fields and meadows in summer, owes its name to the amazing jumps it makes when it extends its hind legs.

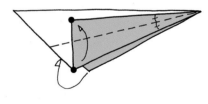

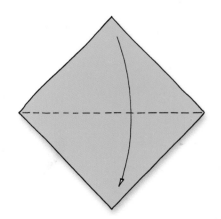

1 Mountain fold a square in half diagonally.

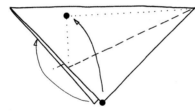

2 Fold the two sides upward on the diagonal as shown, joining the dots and leaving a bit of space from the upper edge.

3 Fold the two sides upward once more.

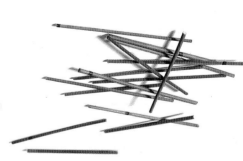

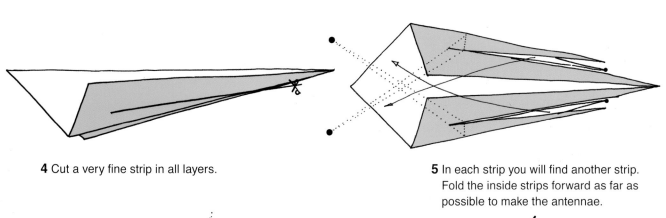

4 Cut a very fine strip in all layers.

5 In each strip you will find another strip. Fold the inside strips forward as far as possible to make the antennae.

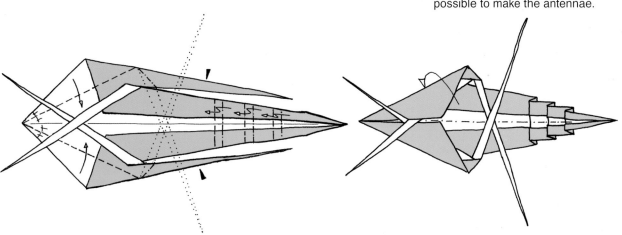

6 Fold the two other strips in a reverse fold (see p. 13) after prefolding. On the left side, fold the edges toward the center. On the right side, make a series of pleat folds.

7 Mountain fold the model in half.

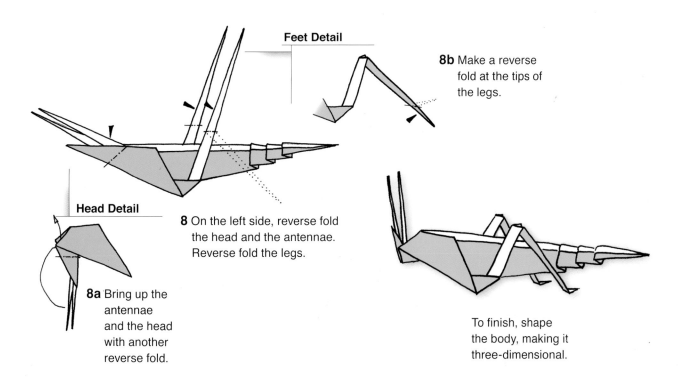

Feet Detail

8b Make a reverse fold at the tips of the legs.

Head Detail

8 On the left side, reverse fold the head and the antennae. Reverse fold the legs.

8a Bring up the antennae and the head with another reverse fold.

To finish, shape the body, making it three-dimensional.

Cube

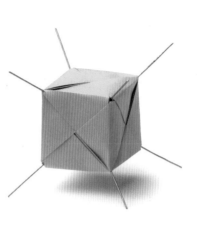

▶▶ Intermediate

This model is made with six different colored pieces of paper. You can attach several cubes together with the help of straws or rods, either inserted right through the cube or along the edges.

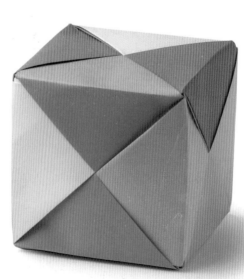

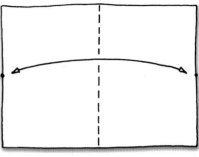

1 Start with an A4 or A6 sheet (see p. 16). Crease the center.

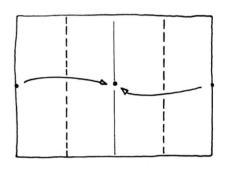

2 Fold the edges to the center crease.

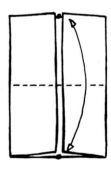

3 Crease the center.

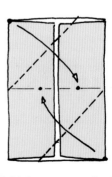

4 Fold the corners along the center crease …

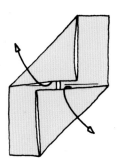

5 … like this, then unfold the corners.

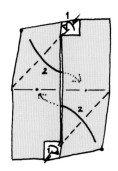

6 Fold the small corners inside (1), then slide the two corners between the two layers (2) …

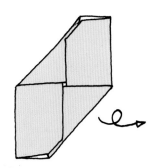

7 … like this, then turn it over.

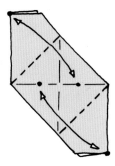

8 Make two creases by joining the points. This creates the assembly tabs. Make five more units in the same way.

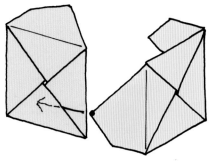

9 Slide the tab of the first unit between the layers of the second unit.

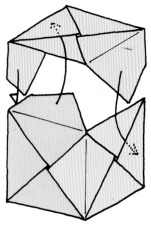

10 Slide in the two tabs of the third unit like the previous ones, then rotate the model.

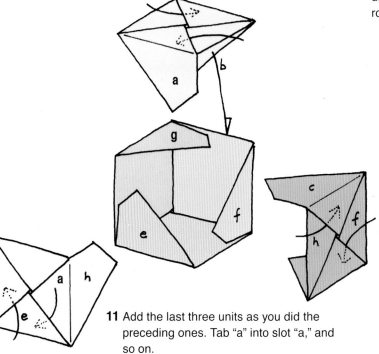

11 Add the last three units as you did the preceding ones. Tab "a" into slot "a," and so on.

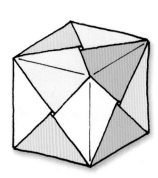

12 Have fun making cubes of different sizes.

Fancy Star and Ball

▶▶ Intermediate

This star needs just a bit of patience and a little attention to detail to make a beautiful creation.

The Star

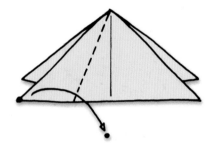

1 First make a cube (see p. 112) from A5 paper. Set aside for now. From a 7 inch square, fold a waterbomb base (see p. 12), then fold down one side along the center crease.

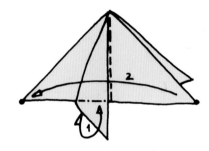

2 Mountain crease the lower point (1), then fold one layer to the left (2).

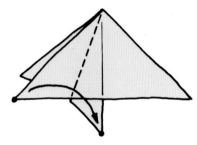

3 Fold the second side like the first.

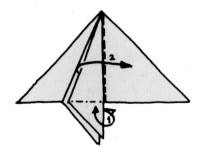

4 Mountain crease the lower point (1), then fold the layer back to the right (2) …

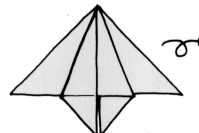

5 … like this, then turn it over.

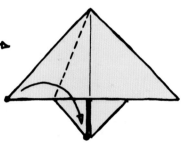

6 Repeat the same operation for the third layer.

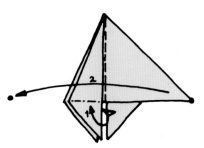

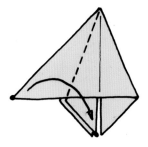

7 Crease the bottom point (1), then turn the last layer to the left (2).

8 Repeat the operation one last time.

9 Crease the last point (1) and fold the layer back to the right (2).

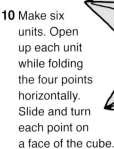

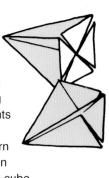

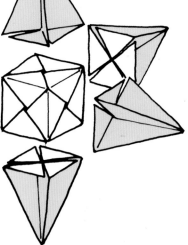

10 Make six units. Open up each unit while folding the four points horizontally. Slide and turn each point on a face of the cube.

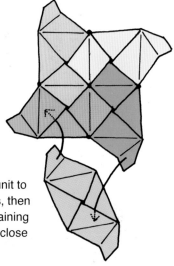

11 To hold it in place more permanently, you can glue the units together.

The Ball

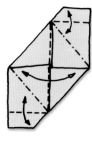

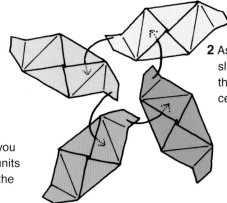

1 To make the ball, you need to make 12 units like you made for the cube (steps 1–8, pp. 112–13). Valley crease the diagonal of the central square and mountain crease the two edges of the square. Finally, valley crease the assembly tabs.

2 Assemble four units by sliding each tab under the upper layer of the central square.

3 Add a third unit to the free tabs, then use the remaining four units to close the ball.

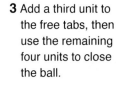

4 You can make balls of different sizes by using paper of A4 proportions (see p. 16).

Penguin

A penguin looks like a man in a tuxedo when standing up, but its waddling walk makes us laugh.

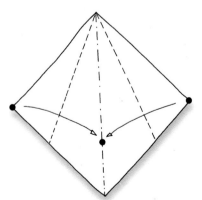

1 Crease the diagonal of a square sheet of paper. Then fold the two edges to the crease.

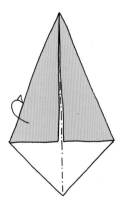

2 Fold in half to the right.

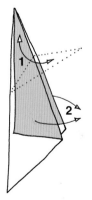

3 Fold the point as shown. Then unfold the head (1), and open the sides out (2).

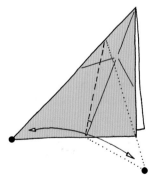

4 Crease by folding the whole left side as shown, then open completely.

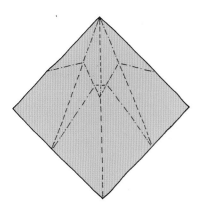

5 Before refolding, put the creases in mountain and valley folds, as shown.

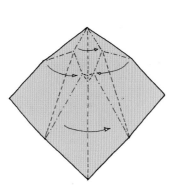

6 Begin to refold.

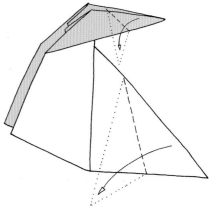

7 Fold the right point to the left. For the beak, valley fold the corner.

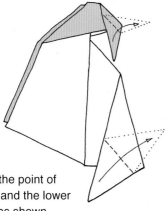

8 Bring up the point of the beak and the lower triangle, as shown.

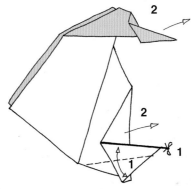

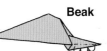

9 Cut on the solid line, crease at the base (1), and unfold the beak and the base (2).

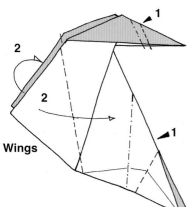

Wings

10 For the beak and the right point, open and make reverse folds (1). Valley fold the left side on each surface to make the wings (2).

Details

Beak

10a Make the beak narrower by folding half to the inside. Fold the tip.

Feet

10b To bring out the feet, fold to the inside on existing creases. Then put the feet flat. Make the penguin three-dimensional from the inside.

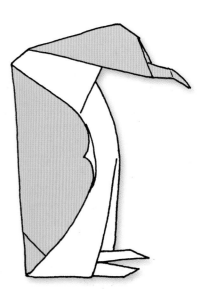

Cat

▶▶▶ Advanced

The cat is the domesticated member of the feline family. It seeks out human companionship now and again and even lets itself be stroked when it feels like it. Then, on a whim, it runs away a moment later.

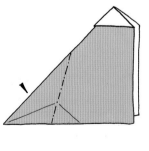

Body

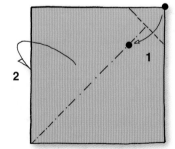

1 Start with a square slightly larger than the one you will use for the head. With the color side up, valley fold a small corner down (1), then mountain fold in two along the diagonal (2).

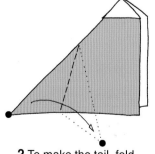

2 To make the tail, fold the point down.

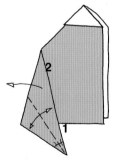

3 Fold the point in half (1), then unfold (2).

4 Reverse fold on existing crease.

118

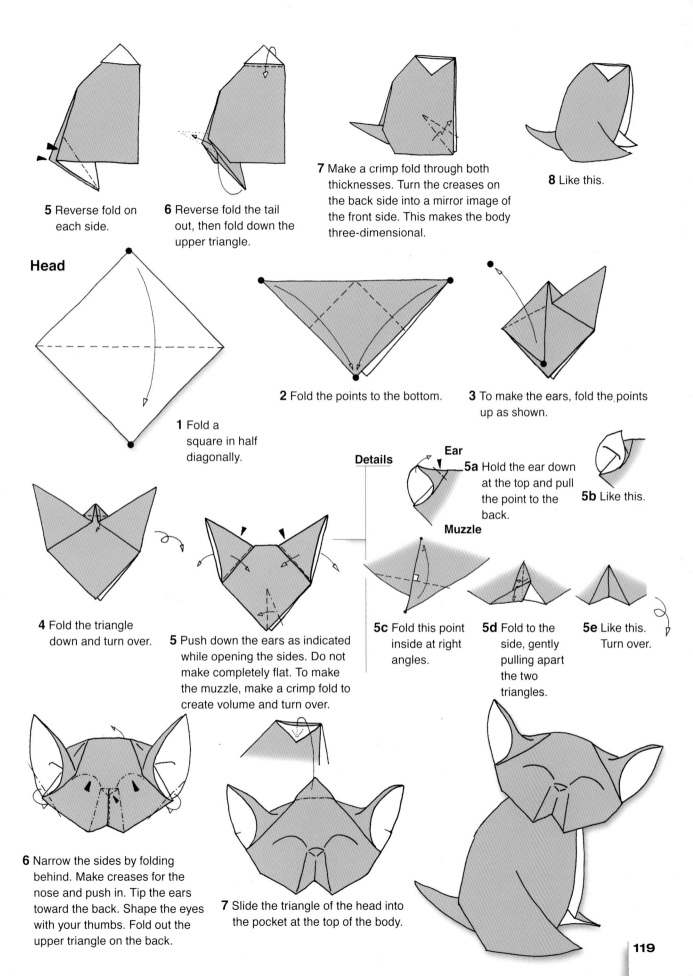

5 Reverse fold on each side.

6 Reverse fold the tail out, then fold down the upper triangle.

7 Make a crimp fold through both thicknesses. Turn the creases on the back side into a mirror image of the front side. This makes the body three-dimensional.

8 Like this.

Head

1 Fold a square in half diagonally.

2 Fold the points to the bottom.

3 To make the ears, fold the points up as shown.

4 Fold the triangle down and turn over.

5 Push down the ears as indicated while opening the sides. Do not make completely flat. To make the muzzle, make a crimp fold to create volume and turn over.

Details

Ear

5a Hold the ear down at the top and pull the point to the back.

5b Like this.

Muzzle

5c Fold this point inside at right angles.

5d Fold to the side, gently pulling apart the two triangles.

5e Like this. Turn over.

6 Narrow the sides by folding behind. Make creases for the nose and push in. Tip the ears toward the back. Shape the eyes with your thumbs. Fold out the upper triangle on the back.

7 Slide the triangle of the head into the pocket at the top of the body.

Squadron

▶▶▶ Advanced

This model reminds one of the folding technique used in Schoolboy, which was explained on page 104. It's a traditional Chinese model. Assembling a couple of small airplanes on top of the big one produces an overall effect of power to the whole group.

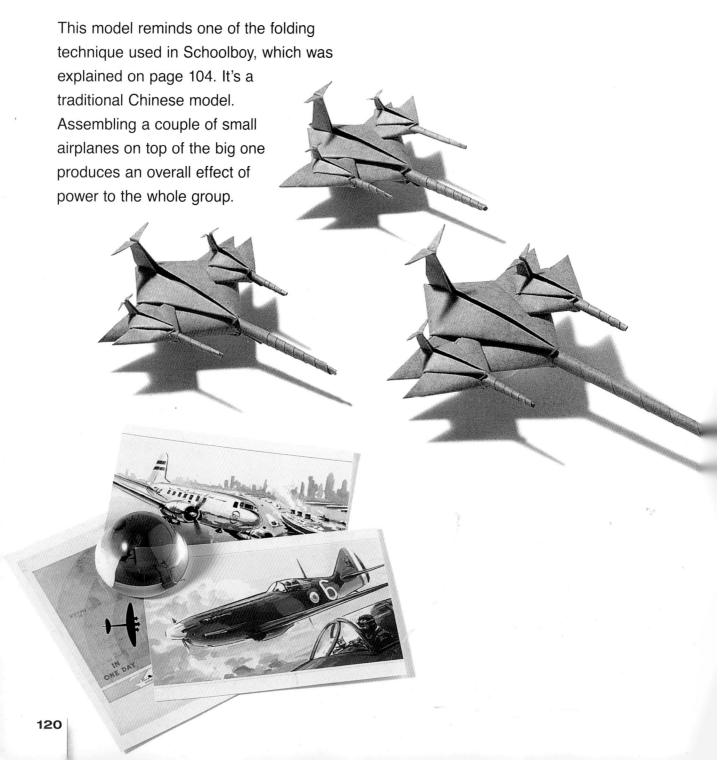

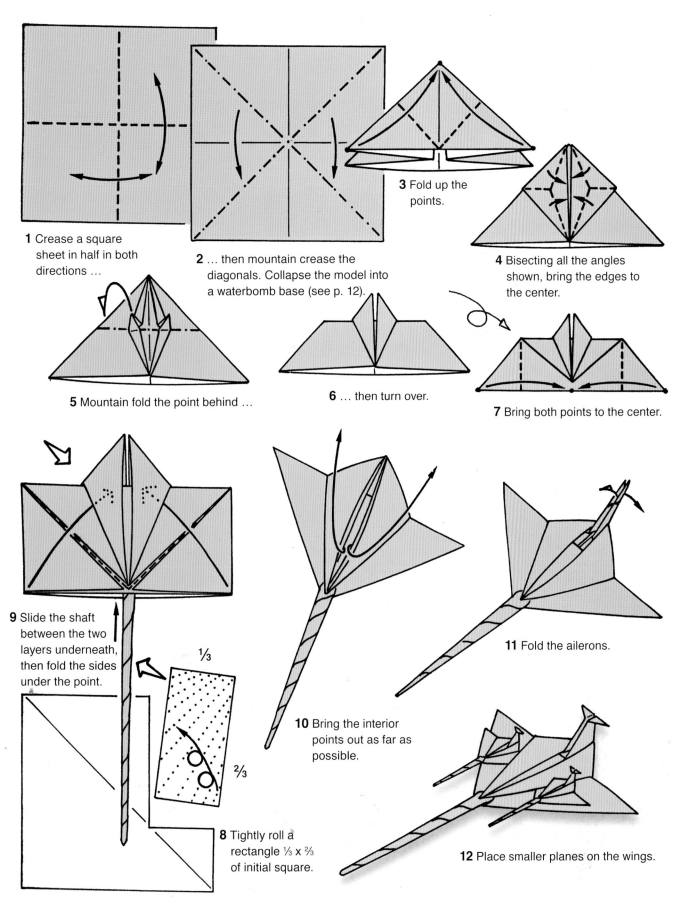

1 Crease a square sheet in half in both directions …

2 … then mountain crease the diagonals. Collapse the model into a waterbomb base (see p. 12).

3 Fold up the points.

4 Bisecting all the angles shown, bring the edges to the center.

5 Mountain fold the point behind …

6 … then turn over.

7 Bring both points to the center.

8 Tightly roll a rectangle ⅓ x ⅔ of initial square.

⅓

⅔

9 Slide the shaft between the two layers underneath, then fold the sides under the point.

10 Bring the interior points out as far as possible.

11 Fold the ailerons.

12 Place smaller planes on the wings.

Bull

▶▶▶ Advanced

Throughout the centuries and in many civilizations, the bull has been revered for its strength. In Roman times, it enlivened the circus games, a custom that continues to this day in the south of France and in Spain. The bull you find here is quite harmless.

Body

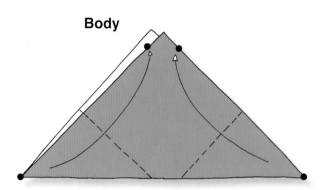

1 Fold a square (slightly larger than the one for the head) in half diagonally, then fold the points up leaving a space as shown.

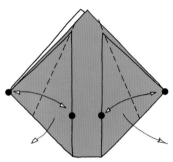

2 Fold through all layers while folding the points in two. Unfold.

3 Make reverse folds on both sides.

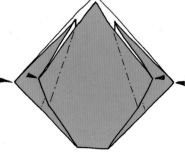

4 Following existing creases, make reverse folds on the four corners.

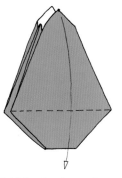

5 Fold the top layer down.

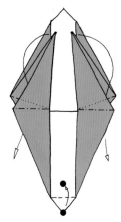

6 Bring the two points down with reverse folds, leaving them slightly open. Fold up the small triangle at the bottom. And invert.

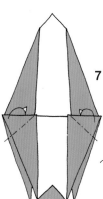

7 Fold the corners behind, then turn model over.

8 Pinch the upper point. This will receive the head.

Head

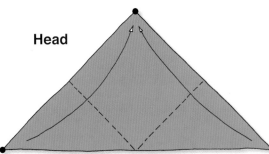

1 Bring the points of a half-square to the top, joining the points.

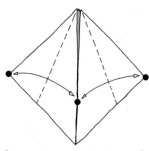

2 Fold and unfold edges of all layers to center.

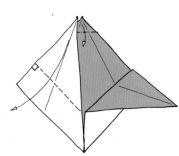

3 Fold down the points to the outside, noting the right angle, then fold down the tip of the triangle.

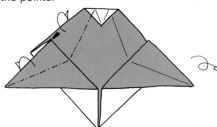

4 Mountain fold the left side on existing creases, then turn over.

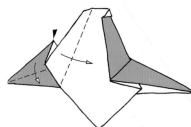

5 Fold the other side in the same manner.

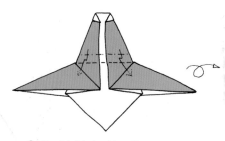

6 Pleat fold, tucking the corners between the layers, then turn over and invert.

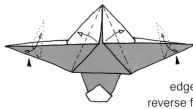

7 Fold the raw edges to the outside edge. To make the horns, reverse fold the tips.

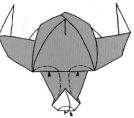

Head Details

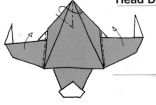

8 Crease along the bottom edge of the horns; then make the head three-dimensional by folding as indicated, tucking the left side under the right-side layer.

8a Fold the point that sticks out behind. Leave this point slightly open to help hold the head on the body.

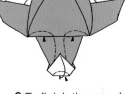

9 To finish the muzzle, curve the bottom and curl the tip down. Shape the eyes with your thumbs on the horizontal edge. Shape the muzzle vertically also. Place the head on the body as shown in step 8a.

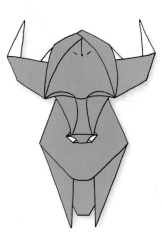

123

Hen

))) Advanced

In the farmyard, hens go about their business pecking at
seeds, snapping at small insects, and sitting on their eggs.

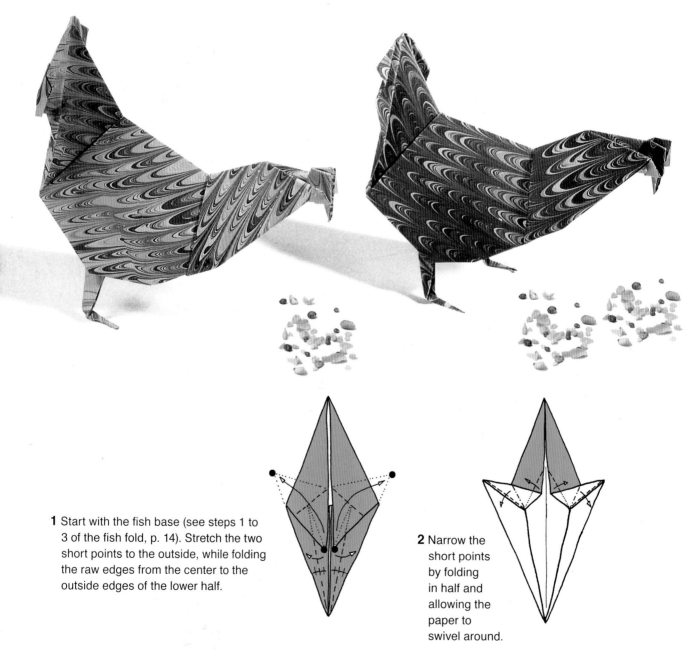

1 Start with the fish base (see steps 1 to
3 of the fish fold, p. 14). Stretch the two
short points to the outside, while folding
the raw edges from the center to the
outside edges of the lower half.

2 Narrow the
short points
by folding
in half and
allowing the
paper to
swivel around.

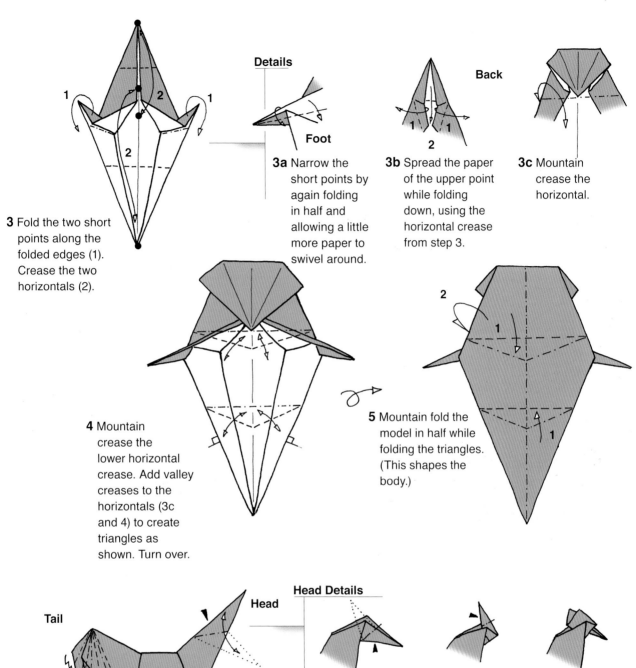

3 Fold the two short points along the folded edges (1). Crease the two horizontals (2).

Details

Foot

3a Narrow the short points by again folding in half and allowing a little more paper to swivel around.

3b Spread the paper of the upper point while folding down, using the horizontal crease from step 3.

Back

3c Mountain crease the horizontal.

4 Mountain crease the lower horizontal crease. Add valley creases to the horizontals (3c and 4) to create triangles as shown. Turn over.

5 Mountain fold the model in half while folding the triangles. (This shapes the body.)

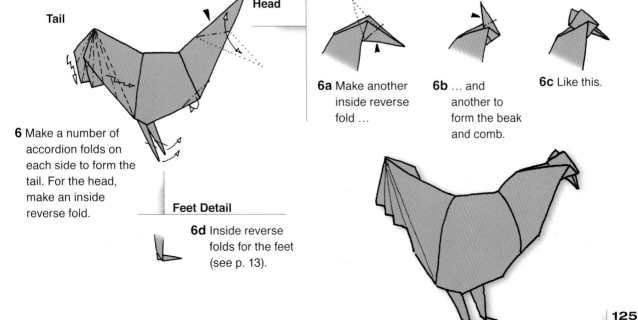

Tail

Head

Head Details

6 Make a number of accordion folds on each side to form the tail. For the head, make an inside reverse fold.

6a Make another inside reverse fold …

6b … and another to form the beak and comb.

6c Like this.

Feet Detail

6d Inside reverse folds for the feet (see p. 13).

Horse

▶▶▶ Advanced

To make this horse stand on its hind legs, all you need to do is fold the points again and find the balance point.

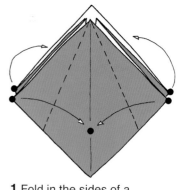

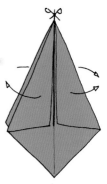

1 Fold in the sides of a preliminary base (see p. 11).

2 Cut along the heavy line only as far as the folded edge, then unfold.

3 Fold down the points on both sides, front and back.

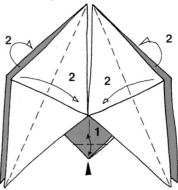

4 Sink the base after prefolding (1) (see p. 11). Fold the sides along the existing creases (2).

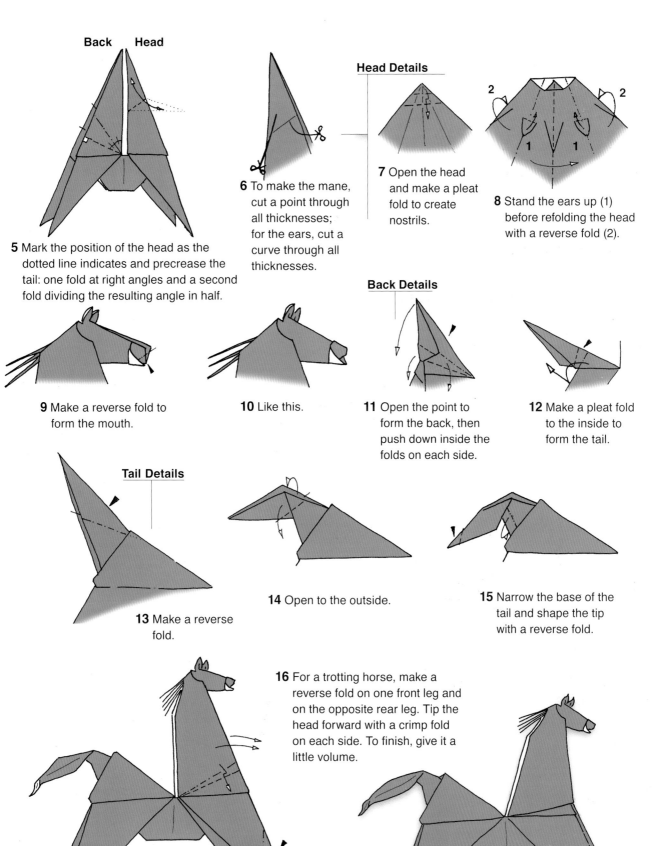

Back   Head

5 Mark the position of the head as the dotted line indicates and precrease the tail: one fold at right angles and a second fold dividing the resulting angle in half.

6 To make the mane, cut a point through all thicknesses; for the ears, cut a curve through all thicknesses.

Head Details

7 Open the head and make a pleat fold to create nostrils.

8 Stand the ears up (1) before refolding the head with a reverse fold (2).

9 Make a reverse fold to form the mouth.

10 Like this.

Back Details

11 Open the point to form the back, then push down inside the folds on each side.

12 Make a pleat fold to the inside to form the tail.

Tail Details

13 Make a reverse fold.

14 Open to the outside.

15 Narrow the base of the tail and shape the tip with a reverse fold.

16 For a trotting horse, make a reverse fold on one front leg and on the opposite rear leg. Tip the head forward with a crimp fold on each side. To finish, give it a little volume.

Sound Barrier

▶▶▶ Advanced

This paper-folding was designed to go along naturally with the proportions of an A4 piece of paper. It proceeds in logical steps of folding and results in this beautiful plane. (To get the proportion of an A4 sheet, trim ⅝ inch from the width of a letter-sized sheet.)

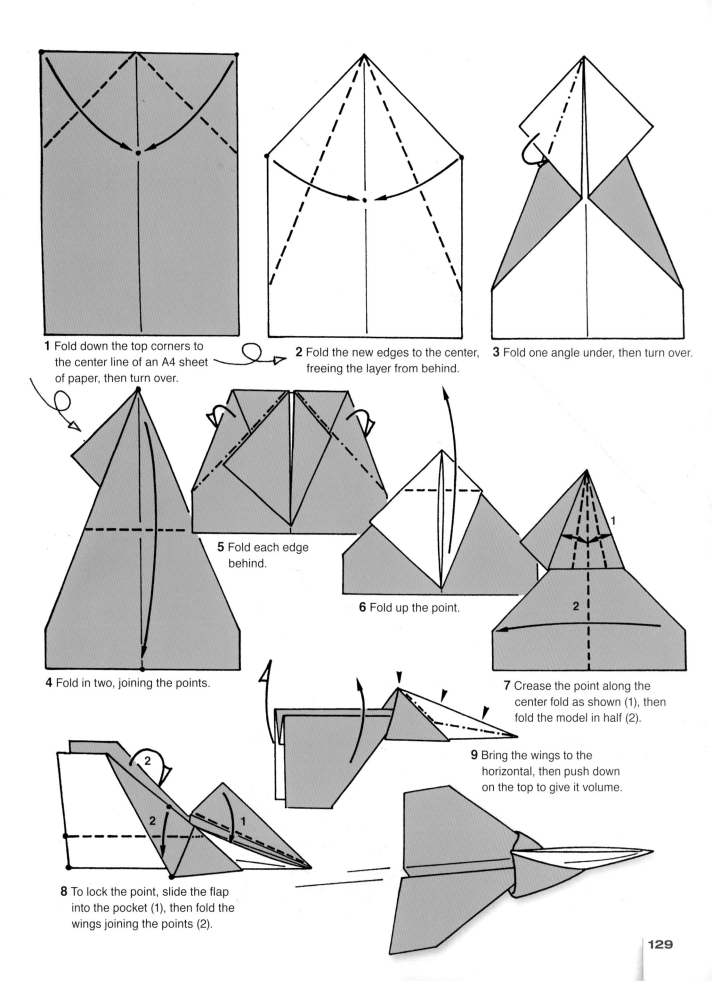

1 Fold down the top corners to the center line of an A4 sheet of paper, then turn over.

2 Fold the new edges to the center, freeing the layer from behind.

3 Fold one angle under, then turn over.

4 Fold in two, joining the points.

5 Fold each edge behind.

6 Fold up the point.

7 Crease the point along the center fold as shown (1), then fold the model in half (2).

8 To lock the point, slide the flap into the pocket (1), then fold the wings joining the points (2).

9 Bring the wings to the horizontal, then push down on the top to give it volume.

Frog

▶▶▶ Advanced

Frogs love to congregate at the edges of ponds at nightfall to organize croaking concerts that herald rain and sometimes fine weather. Their fingertips act like suction cups, allowing them to climb just about anywhere without falling down.

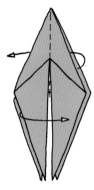

1 Start with the frog base (see p. 14) and fold over one layer on each side.

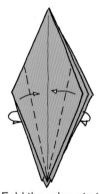

2 Fold the edges to the center on each side.

3 Fold over layers on each side to find sides that look like step 2, and fold the sides in as in step 2 on both sides.

4 Fold over one layer on each side.

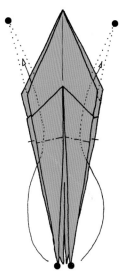

5 To make the front legs, reverse fold the points of the upper layer to the front.

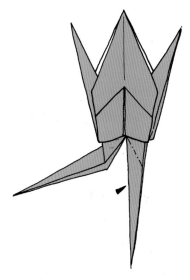

6 To make the rear legs, make inside reverse folds (see p. 13) as on the left.

7 Make reverse folds in front and rear legs as shown on the left.

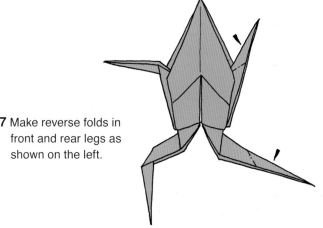

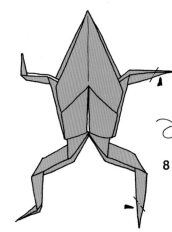

8 Inside reverse the tips of all four legs and turn model over.

9 You need to stop here and inflate the frog from the rear. You can also add beads between the layers as shown for eyes and fold the front tip under. Finally, cut the tips of the legs in half.

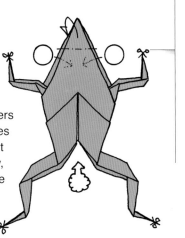

Feet Details

9a Then open the tips of the legs to cut the points again to make five toes.

Eagle

>>> Advanced

The eagle is a powerful and majestic bird that soars on high, spotting prey with its sharp eyesight. It generally carries its catch between its talons several miles in the air. The eagle presented here can hold a small object between its feet or can balance on a finger.

1 Starting with a waterbomb base (see p. 12), fold one point on each side down along the center crease, then unfold.

2 Open the point and squash fold it symmetrically. Repeat on other side.

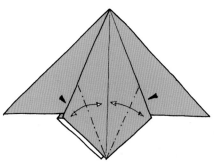

3 Make creases by folding edges to the central crease. Unfold and make them reverse folds.

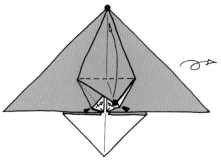

4 Fold the resulting point up to meet the top point, flattening the model, then turn over.

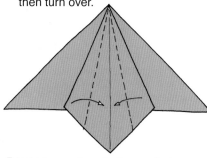

5 Fold long edges to the central crease.

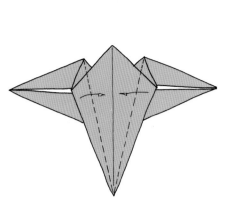

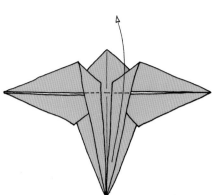

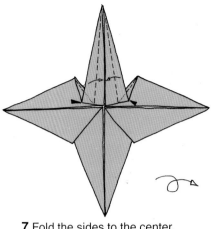

5 Valley fold the sides from angle to angle.

6 Fold up the narrow point.

7 Fold the sides to the center, flattening the indicated corners. Turn over.

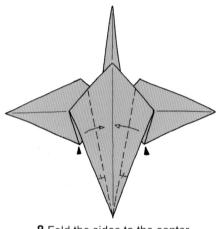

Neck Detail

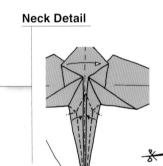

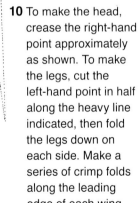

8 Fold the sides to the center, allowing the indicated corners to spread.

9 Valley fold the sides of the point to the center while mountain folding the point in half. Pinch the paper at the base of the wings and fold model in half.

10 To make the head, crease the right-hand point approximately as shown. To make the legs, cut the left-hand point in half along the heavy line indicated, then fold the legs down on each side. Make a series of crimp folds along the leading edge of each wing.

Head Details

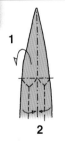

1

2

10a Open the point of the head and mountain fold the upper triangle (1). Fold the edges to the center and pinch together at the base of the head to make it lie flat (2).

10b To make the crest, cut a fine strip on each side and fold them straight back. Crimp fold to make the beak.

10c Reverse fold the corners indicated on each side to shape the face.

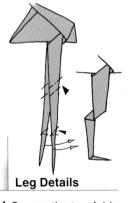

Leg Details

11 Crease the two folds indicated in the middle of the leg. Use these creases to make a crimp fold as shown. For the feet, crimp fold to the horizontal (see p. 15).

Star Cluster

▶▶▶ Advanced

Starting with this basic module, you can create a series of stars, each more complex in design, to decorate your room or a holiday table.

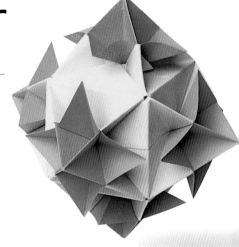

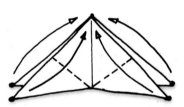

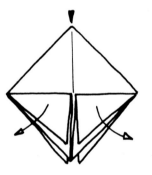

The Star

1 Start with a square and make a waterbomb base (see p. 12), then fold the points up front and back.

Enlarged View

2 Fold the four points down.

3 Unfold completely, then push in the center to change the direction of the folds.

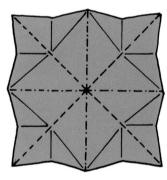

4 Fold along the creases to make a preliminary base (see p. 11).

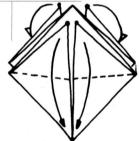

5 Pinch the point in half by creasing as shown (1), then bring up the flap (2). Repeat this step on the other side.

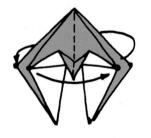

6 Fold one flap to the right, then on the back fold one flap to the left. Repeat step 5 for the other two faces.

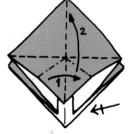

7 The star will be completed once it is joined to the base.

The Base

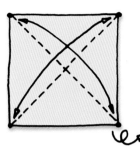 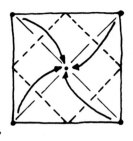 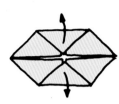 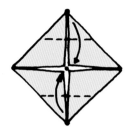 

1 Start with a square the same size as used for the star. Crease the diagonals by joining the points, then turn it over.

2 Fold the corners to the center.

3 Fold in the upper and lower corners.

4 Unfold the two corners.

5 Open while refolding the points to the center.

Enlarged View

6 Bring the four triangles to the vertical folds.

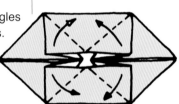

Assembly

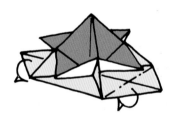

1 Slide each of the four points of the star into the triangles of the base. To make the assembly easier, you can partially unfold the base.

2 Mountain fold the sides.

3 This star with its base can be used to decorate a holiday table.

4 You can also cross two units back to back, then fold the sides into each other to close the model. By assembling six units in the same way, into a cube, you can make the large star cluster on the opposite page.

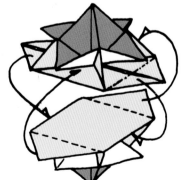

What's This?

▶▶▶ Advanced

What is this? Is it an observatory? A space vessel? You decide. Use your imagination.

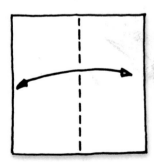

1 Start with a square the same size used for the star (p. 136). Crease the center.

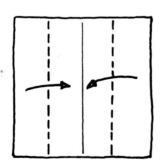

2 Fold the sides.

3 Fold in the four corners.

4 Unfold completely.

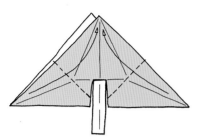

5 Fold the points to the top.

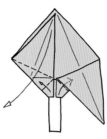

6 Valley fold the two points down to the top of the slit for the tail as shown on the right, and fold the small flaps under.

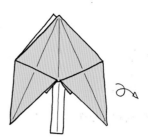

7 Like this. Turn over

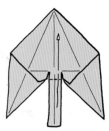

8 Fold up the tail.

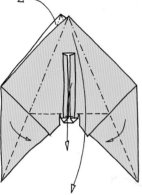

9 Open the two layers, folding the top layer toward the front.

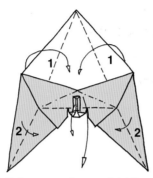

10 At the same time, refold the sides on the existing creases (1) and fold the lower points in two to make the model lie flat (2).

Tail Details

8a Fold the sides to the center crease and make the small triangle at the bottom flat, as on the left.

8b Like this.

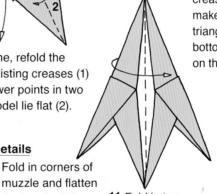

11 Fold in two.

12 Make crimp folds on both sides and tuck under the layers of the leg as shown.

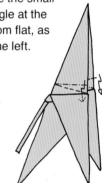

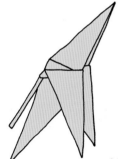

13 Like this.

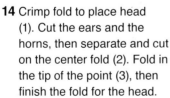

14 Crimp fold to place head (1). Cut the ears and the horns, then separate and cut on the center fold (2). Fold in the tip of the point (3), then finish the fold for the head.

Head Details

14a Fold in corners of muzzle and flatten the head a little.

14b Like this.

Tail Details

14c Fold the sides up on the long diagonal.

14d Fold out the bottom end of each side.

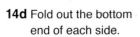

14e Like this. Gently curve the tail and shape the body and neck.

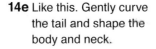

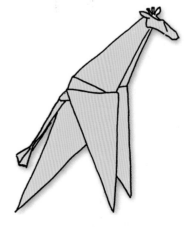

Panther

DDD Advanced

This feline, which looks like a big cat, owns several passports. In Africa its name is leopard, while in the Americas it is known as a jaguar.

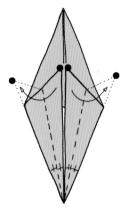

1 Start with a fish base (see p. 14). Open to the outside.

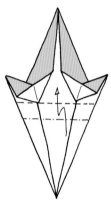

2 Pleat fold.

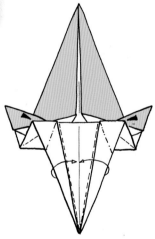

3 Narrow the lower point by folding the edges to the center fold and make it lie flat.

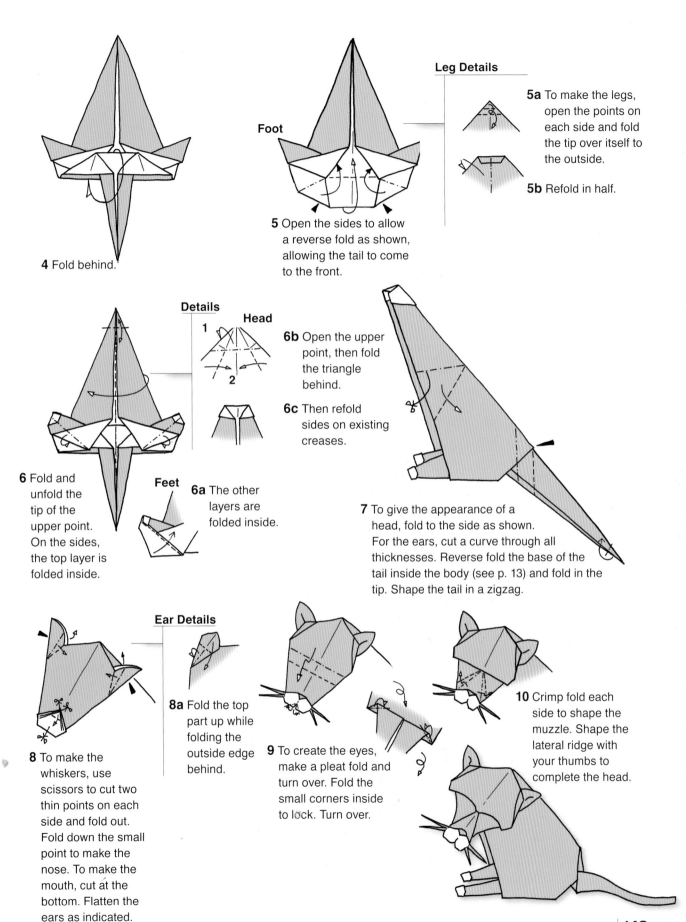

4 Fold behind.

Foot

5 Open the sides to allow a reverse fold as shown, allowing the tail to come to the front.

Leg Details

5a To make the legs, open the points on each side and fold the tip over itself to the outside.

5b Refold in half.

Details

Head

1

2

6b Open the upper point, then fold the triangle behind.

6c Then refold sides on existing creases.

6 Fold and unfold the tip of the upper point. On the sides, the top layer is folded inside.

Feet

6a The other layers are folded inside.

7 To give the appearance of a head, fold to the side as shown. For the ears, cut a curve through all thicknesses. Reverse fold the base of the tail inside the body (see p. 13) and fold in the tip. Shape the tail in a zigzag.

Ear Details

8 To make the whiskers, use scissors to cut two thin points on each side and fold out. Fold down the small point to make the nose. To make the mouth, cut at the bottom. Flatten the ears as indicated.

8a Fold the top part up while folding the outside edge behind.

9 To create the eyes, make a pleat fold and turn over. Fold the small corners inside to lock. Turn over.

10 Crimp fold each side to shape the muzzle. Shape the lateral ridge with your thumbs to complete the head.

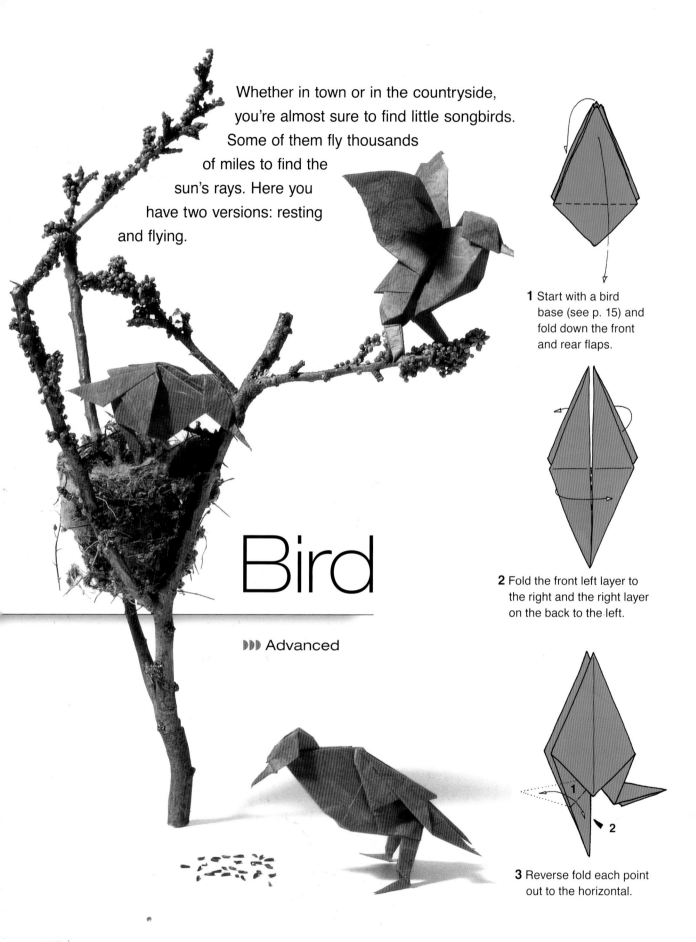

Whether in town or in the countryside, you're almost sure to find little songbirds. Some of them fly thousands of miles to find the sun's rays. Here you have two versions: resting and flying.

Bird

▶▶▶ Advanced

1 Start with a bird base (see p. 15) and fold down the front and rear flaps.

2 Fold the front left layer to the right and the right layer on the back to the left.

3 Reverse fold each point out to the horizontal.

Resting Bird

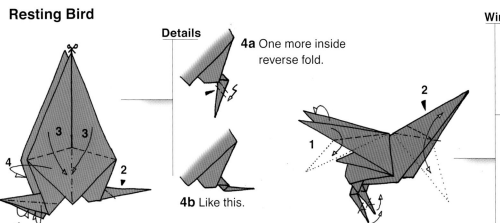

Details

4a One more inside reverse fold.

4b Like this.

5a Fold the wings along the back.

Head Details

5b Pull the point up in another reverse fold.

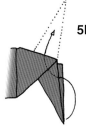

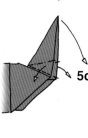

5c Bring the point down while opening the sides.

5d Hold the point with your thumb and forefinger and tip up the point at the back of the head.

5e Crimp fold to form beak (see p. 15).

5f Thin the beak by folding the edges inside.

4 Start with the legs: narrow the two points by folding in half to the inside (1), then make inside reverse folds on each leg (2). Continue folding the legs by following steps 4a and 4b. Cut the top flap in half along center crease, folding down the resulting two points (3). Fold the model in half along the center crease (4).

5 Fold the wings to lie along the back of the model (1). Crimp fold the legs to make the feet (see p. 15). Make a reverse fold for the head (2).

Flying Bird

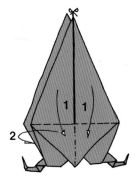

Details

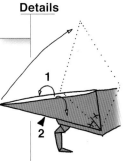

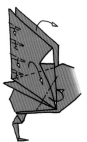

4 To make a bird with wings spread, cut the top point in half, then fold the wings (1). Mountain fold in half along vertical axis (2).

4a Open each point (1) and squash fold vertically (2).

4b Fold one side. Repeat on back.

4c Fold the lower corner under. Fold wing down along back of model and make a series of small crimp folds on the trailing edge to curve the wing. Repeat on the other side.

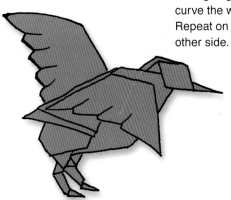

Stealth

▶▶▶ Advanced

Stephen Weiss created this model, which he called
Level Track Delta. The elegant design with its
swept-back wings gives this
plane perfect stability.

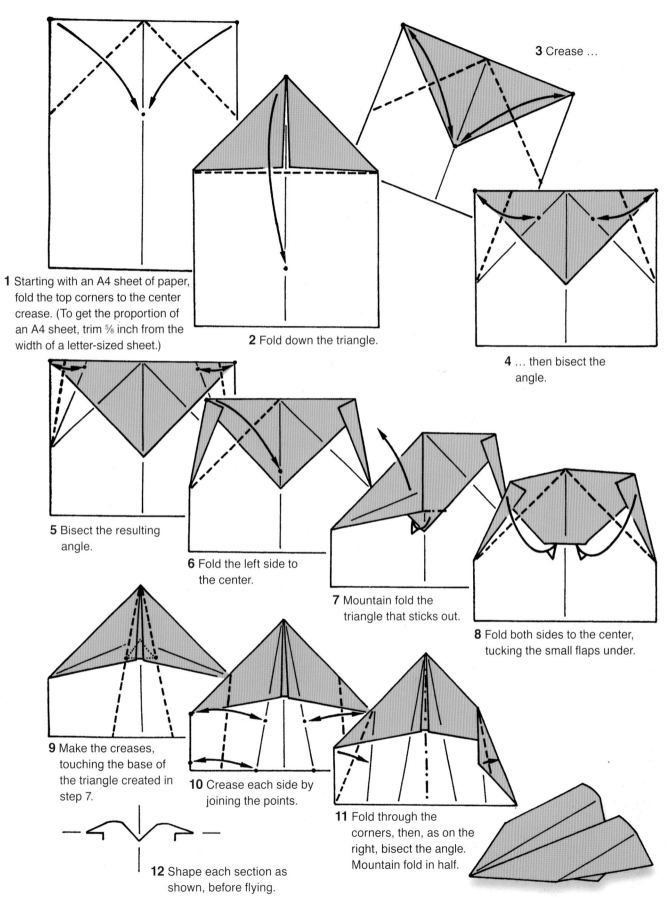

1 Starting with an A4 sheet of paper, fold the top corners to the center crease. (To get the proportion of an A4 sheet, trim ⅝ inch from the width of a letter-sized sheet.)

2 Fold down the triangle.

3 Crease …

4 … then bisect the angle.

5 Bisect the resulting angle.

6 Fold the left side to the center.

7 Mountain fold the triangle that sticks out.

8 Fold both sides to the center, tucking the small flaps under.

9 Make the creases, touching the base of the triangle created in step 7.

10 Crease each side by joining the points.

11 Fold through the corners, then, as on the right, bisect the angle. Mountain fold in half.

12 Shape each section as shown, before flying.

Designs for Airplanes

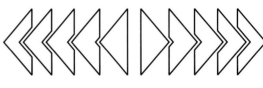

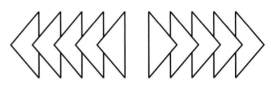

Here are some illustrations that you can reproduce with tracing paper and color to decorate your airplanes. You could also photocopy them, cut them out and glue them onto your models — but doing that may mean compromising the aerodynamic qualities of your paper airplanes. You'll have to make some trial flights.

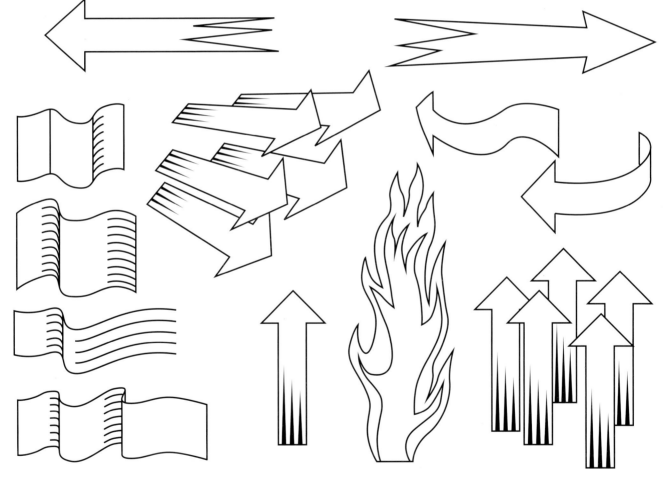

Here are some examples in color for you to decorate your planes.